Kev, the Care Home Cat

Dawn Milsom

Inspired by a True Story

The Unforgettable Account of the Scruffy Stray
Who Taught an Entire Nursing Home How To Love Again

Copyright © 2025 by Dawn Milsom

All rights reserved.

No part of this book may be reproduced, stored in a retrieval system, or transmitted in any form or by any means—electronic, mechanical, photocopying, recording, or otherwise—without the prior written permission of the publisher, except for brief quotations in critical reviews or articles.

ISBN 978-1-918219-22-7

First Edition: 2025
Published by: Cosmic Jive Publishing

www.cosmicjivepublishing.com

For permissions and inquiries, contact:
info@cosmicjivepublishing.com

This narrative is created for the purpose of the story. Names, characters, events, and dialogue are reconstructed or are products of dramatic license. Any resemblance to actual persons, living or dead, is purely coincidental.

For Kev.

Impossible to forget.

Thank you for every rumbling purr.

Prologue

I never expected to write a book about a cat. I'm a care home manager, not a writer, and before Kev, I would have told you I was more of a dog person anyway. But some stories insist on being told, and this one has been weighing on my chest for some time now, demanding to be shared.

This is the story of how a scruffy ginger tom changed everything at Rivermead Care Home in a small market town in the West Midlands. It's about the residents who lived there, the staff who cared for them, and one cat who somehow understood what we all needed before we knew ourselves.

I'm the one who was there. Who watched it all unfold. Who kept the Good Book—a spiral journal with a cheerful rainbow on the cover, where I recorded not the failures and incidents, but the small miracles that Kev was creating.

So here it is. Kev's story. Our story. The story of how one scruffy ginger stray taught an entire building full of people.

How to care when caring will cost you everything.

How to show up anyway.

I've changed some names and details at the request of families or for legal reasons, but everything else is exactly as it happened. The good bits, the hard bits, and all the messy, complicated, beautiful bits in between.

This is the story of how I learned to do my job properly. Not from protocols or inspections or best practice guidelines, but from a stray who understood something essential that I'd forgotten: that care isn't about systems. It's about showing up.

—Dawn Milsom, October 2025

THE FIRST VISIT

The first time I saw Kev, I was having the worst day of my career.

It was a Monday in December, cold and drizzling and unrelenting in that particularly British way that seeps into your bones and settles there, promising months more of the same.

I'd been manager of Rivermead for eighteen months—long enough to feel the weight of every decision, every mistake, pressing down on me. I was questioning everything, especially whether I was cut out for this job.

The morning had started badly and deteriorated from there. The CQC inspection team had arrived unannounced first thing, clipboards at the ready, and spent three hours picking apart our medication management system. Not catastrophically—no one had been harmed, no serious errors made—but enough discrepancies to warrant a "requires improvement" rating. Enough to make me feel like a failure.

Then Julie Jenkins, one of our best care assistants, had handed in her notice. "It's not you," she'd said, which is what people always say when it absolutely is you. "I've been offered more money at the nursing home in town. I can't afford to stay here on these wages."

I couldn't argue. I couldn't offer her more. The budget was what it was, stretched so thin you could see through it.

And then Phyllis in room twelve had fallen during the night shift. She wasn't seriously hurt—bruised hip, shaken confidence—but her daughter had arrived at one o'clock sharp and spent forty minutes in my office, her voice rising with each sentence, hurling accusations about negligence and inadequate staffing and how her mother deserved better than this, how she was considering legal action, how she'd tell everyone she knew to avoid Rivermead.

I'd apologised. Explained our fall prevention protocols. Showed her the incident report, the immediate response times, the care plan adjustments we'd already implemented. None of it mattered. Her mother had fallen, and someone needed to be blamed.

That someone was me.

By half past two, I was standing in the car park, ostensibly checking my phone but actually just trying not to cry.

The rain had stopped but everything was damp and grey. Christmas lights twinkled half-heartedly in neighbouring windows, their cheerfulness feeling like an accusation. I was thinking about going home, running a bath, and possibly never coming back.

That's when I heard it.

"Mrow."

"Mrow."

Not a meow. *A mrow.* There's a difference.

I looked down. Sitting by my feet, as if he'd been there all along waiting patiently for me to notice, was the scruffiest cat I'd ever seen.

He was ginger—or had been, once. Now he was more of a faded orange, with white patches on his chest and paws that might have once been pristine but were currently the colour of old dishwater. One ear had a chunk missing from the tip as if something with teeth had had a go at it and he'd escaped but not unscathed. His tail kinked halfway down at an odd angle. And he was looking up at me with enormous amber eyes that somehow conveyed both supreme confidence and mild disappointment in my life choices.

"Hello," I said stupidly, because what else do you say to a cat who's appeared at exactly the moment you're contemplating giving up?

"Mrow," he said again, and headbutted my shin with surprising force.

I'm not ashamed to admit that I crouched down right there in the car park and burst into tears, one hand on this random cat's head while he purred like a small motorcycle.

He just stood there, solid and warm and entirely unbothered, occasionally rubbing his face against my wrist as if to say: *Yes, you're upset. That's allowed. Carry on.*

The tarmac was cold and damp beneath my knees, soaking through my trousers. I don't know how long I stayed like that. Five minutes? Ten? Long enough for my knees to protest, for the tears to stop, for my breathing to even out. The cat stayed the entire time, purring steadily.

He stayed. That's when I should have known he was different.

That's how Denise found us a few minutes later.

"Dawn?" She was standing by the door, her healthcare assistant uniform straining slightly across her middle, her kind face creased with concern. "You alright, love?"

I wiped my face with my free hand. "Fine. Just... it's been a day."

"I can see that." She came closer, then stopped. "Bloody hell, is that the ginger tom from up the road?"

"Is he?" I straightened up, and immediately the cat began weaving between my legs in figures of eight.

"Think so. Mrs. Patterson at number forty-three feeds him, but she says he's not really hers. Just shows up whenever he fancies it." Denise bent down and offered her hand. The cat sniffed it, considered, then allowed exactly three strokes before stepping away with dignity intact. "Scruffy bugger, isn't he?"

"He's perfect," I heard myself say.

Denise gave me a look that suggested she was worried about more than just the inspection results. "Why don't you come in, have a cuppa? I'll tell Phyllis's daughter where to stick her complaints if she's still here."

"She left an hour ago."

"Oh. Well then, come have a cuppa anyway."

I followed her inside, and promptly forgot about the cat.

But he didn't forget about us. I didn't realise that day was only the beginning.

***

The cat came back the next day.

I was in the dining room helping with afternoon tea. Pale winter sunlight struggled through the French windows after another rain shower, and the fairy lights draped around the room were already glowing.

Maureen, one of our residents, suddenly gestured towards the garden. "Look—a cat!"

We all turned. Sure enough, there he was, sitting on the patio just outside, tail wrapped neatly around his paws, staring in at us like he was waiting for a table at a restaurant.

"Shoo!" called Joyce from her wheelchair. "Go on, scat!"

The cat did not move.

"I think he wants to come in," said Maureen.

"Absolutely not," I said automatically. "We can't have animals just wandering into a care home. Health and safety."

Even as I said it, I could see residents craning their necks to get a better look. Maureen had the beginnings of a smile on her face—and Maureen rarely smiled. She'd only been with us for a few months, still raw from the loss of her husband of fifty-four years and the enforced sale of their home. Getting a smile from Maureen was like finding a twenty-pound note in an old coat pocket.

"He's a handsome chap," said Arthur, who was ninety-two and mostly blind but apparently could still make out a ginger cat at ten feet.

"Very handsome," agreed Maureen, her smile widening.

The cat lifted one paw and placed it against the glass. It should have looked ridiculous, but somehow it didn't. It looked... purposeful.

"Oh, for heaven's sake," I muttered, and went to open the door. "Just for a minute. Just to see if he's got a collar or anything."

The cat walked in like he owned the place, his tail held high. Not rushed, not skittish—just a calm, measured walk across the threshold and into the dining room where fifteen elderly people were having tea and biscuits. He paused, surveyed the scene, and then made directly for Maureen.

"Oh!" she said, as he jumped—well, hauled himself, really—onto her lap. "Oh my goodness."

He circled once, twice, then settled down, purring.

Maureen's hand hovered over his back like she was afraid he might vanish. Then, slowly, she lowered it and began to stroke him. Her eyes filled with tears.

"We had a ginger cat," she whispered. "Marmalade. He died six years ago. Harold—my husband—he said we were too old for another one, that it wouldn't be fair..." She trailed off, her hand still moving in long strokes down the cat's back.

Nobody said anything. Even Joyce, who'd wanted the cat shooed away, was quiet.

I should have removed him right then. There were protocols, procedures, risk assessments that would need completing before any animal could be in regular contact with residents. But I looked at Maureen's face, at the way her shoulders had softened, at the tears tracking down her cheeks that weren't entirely sad, and I couldn't do it.

"Five minutes," I said quietly. "Then he has to go."

The cat stayed for twenty.

When I finally scooped him up—and he was surprisingly

heavy—he didn't protest. Just looked at me with those amber eyes and mrowed once, as if to say: *I'll be back.*

I carried him outside and set him down on the patio. He sat, licked one paw, and stared at me.

"You can't keep coming here," I told him.

He mrowed again.

"I mean it. We have rules."

He yawned, showing impressive fangs, then stood and trotted off across the lawn toward the hedge that separated us from the residential street beyond.

I watched him go, then went back inside to find Maureen still sitting in the same spot, her hand resting on her lap where the cat had been, a distant smile on her face.

"What a lovely puss," she said softly.

That night, I lay in bed thinking about Maureen's face, about the cat's calm certainty, and about all the reasons it shouldn't happen again.

By morning, I'd stopped arguing with myself and started planning. If there was any chance of making this work safely, I was going to find it—starting with whoever that cat actually belonged to.

***

Mrs. Patterson at number forty-three was delighted to have me knock on her door. The faint aroma of lavender and freshly brewed tea wafted out into her entrance hall, and the warmth of her cat-filled home wrapped around me like a comforting embrace.

"Oh, you mean the ginger boy!" She was about seventy, small but full of energy, dressed in a pink fleece embroidered with cats. "Yes, he's been coming round for... ooh, must be four years now? Maybe five?"

"Do you own him?" I asked hopefully.

"Good Lord, you never own cats! They own you. But I can't exactly say he's *my* cat the way other people might think. He turns up when he feels like it, then off he goes wherever he fancies. I feed him when he shows up, make sure he's got somewhere warm if the weather's bad. Even take him to the vet for his jabs—when he'll let me!"

She added with a twinkle in her eye, "I know he has other people too. Sometimes he comes round smelling of perfume… a right little tart! Mind you," she paused, "I haven't smelled that perfume on him for a while now. Maybe the other owner's away or—" Her voice drifted off. I understood perfectly; it didn't need saying.

She studied me. "Why? Has he been making a nuisance of himself?"

"Not exactly. He's been visiting the care home where I work. Rivermead, just down the—"

"Oh, I know Rivermead! Lovely place. My cousin was there before she passed, must be… ooh.. three years ago now. Barbara Simmons? You might have known her."

I did a quick mental calculation. Before my time, but I nodded politely anyway.

"So the ginger boy's been visiting you, has he?" Mrs. Patterson looked pleased. "That's nice. He's a friendly soul. Very particular about who he spends time with, mind you. He'll ignore you completely if he doesn't like you, but if he does, he's your friend for life."

"Do you know if he's neutered? Had his vaccinations?"

"Oh yes, all that. When he first started coming round, I took him to the vet, thought he might be lost. But no microchip, no one looking for him. Vet said he was about three or four years old, already neutered, generally healthy if a bit scruffy. I paid for his jabs and whatnot—seemed only right if I was going to feed him.

"I put a little note on his collar at first, saying what I was about to do and asking someone to call if it was a problem, and got a reply: *'He's not mine either, only visits, but is much loved. Please take him to the vet as I cannot afford to! L-'* Whoever L was."

"That's very kind of you." I said. "So he's definitely a stray?"

"Well, that's the funny thing. He doesn't act like a stray, does he? Too confident. I think he probably had a home once—maybe the owner died, or moved and couldn't take him. But he's a survivor, that one. Knows how to look after himself, knows which doors to knock on. I'd gladly have him here full-time, but he seems too independent. Maybe he's looking for something else and just scrounges off me until it shows up."

There was no hint of bitterness in her voice—only the quiet mirth of a lady who truly loved and understood cats.

"Do you think... would it be alright if he kept visiting us? The residents at Rivermead, I mean. If he wants to. He really seemed to make a difference yesterday."

Mrs. Patterson's face lit up. "Oh, that would be lovely! He'd probably enjoy it too. Like I said, he's particular about his friends. If he's chosen your lot, that's something special."

"There'd be paperwork," I warned. "I'd need vet records, proof of vaccinations, regular flea treatments..."

"You just tell me what you need, love."

That's how I found myself, three hours later, sitting in my office with a growing file marked "Therapy Cat Programme" and a sense that I was either doing something wonderful or career-endingly stupid.

I spent that evening researching therapy animal programs with the obsessive focus I usually reserved for CQC compliance. Every study I found said the same thing: animals in care settings reduced anxiety, improved mood, increased social interaction, sometimes even improved physical health outcomes.

But they all focused on formal programs. Trained therapy dogs brought in by volunteers. Official visits with risk assessments and insurance and protocols. None of them mentioned a stray cat who'd appointed himself to the position without interview or reference checks.

The vet records arrived by email the next afternoon—Mrs. Patterson was surprisingly tech-savvy. The cat, who apparently had no official name beyond "the ginger boy" or "that tom," was approximately eight years old, neutered, vaccinated against everything relevant, and in generally good health despite his rough appearance.

The vet had added a note: "Friendly temperament. Good with handling. Missing portion of left ear due to unknown trauma (healed). Kinked tail (birth defect or old injury). No apparent pain or mobility issues. Overall: one very lucky stray."

I spent the rest of the week reading guidelines from the Care Quality Commission, and having increasingly surreal conversations with our insurance provider.

"So let me get this straight," said the very patient woman on the phone. "You want to know if you're covered for a cat."

"A visiting cat, yes."

"That you don't own."

"Correct."

"But who would be attending regularly."

"That's the plan."

"And you want to know about public liability if this cat, who isn't owned by anyone, injures a resident or staff member."

"Exactly."

There was a pause. "You know what? I love my job, but this is a new one. Let me talk to my supervisor."

Two hours later, I had my answer: we were covered, provided we had documentation of the cat's health status and a risk assessment on file. It was like the universe was conspiring to make this happen.

The following Monday, exactly one week after our first meeting, the cat returned.

Dawn Milsom

***

The paperwork took longer than I'd expected, but by the next week everything was in place—insurance, vet records, even a risk assessment that made the inspector in my head stop shouting.

So when Kev turned up again, we were ready for him.

"We need to call him something," said Denise.

We were standing in the garden, watching the cat prowl along the bare flower beds, occasionally stopping to sniff something interesting. January had stripped the well-stocked garden bare, leaving skeletal branches against a pale sky.

"Can't keep saying 'the cat' or 'the ginger one.' He needs a proper name."

"What about Marmalade?" suggested Claire, one of the younger care assistants. "Because he's orange?"

"Too obvious," said Denise. "And anyway, that's what Maureen's old cat was called. Might upset her."

"Ginger?"

"Even more obvious."

"Mr. Whiskers?"

We both looked at Claire.

"What? He has whiskers!"

"Absolutely not," I said firmly. "Nothing cutesy."

The cat, as if sensing he was being discussed, abandoned the flower beds and trotted over to us. He sat down and began washing his face with one paw, entirely unconcerned with the identity crisis we were having on his behalf.

"He looks like a Kevin," said Denise suddenly.

I blinked. "A Kevin?"

"Yeah. Look at him. He's got that... Kevin energy. Like someone's uncle who shows up to family parties, has a laugh, few drinks, goes home. Friendly but not too friendly. Knows everyone but belongs to no one."

I looked at the cat. He looked back at me, one paw

suspended in mid-wash.

"Kevin," I said experimentally.

"Mrow," said the cat.

"Kev for short," added Denise.

"Kev," I repeated.

The cat stood up, stretched elaborately, and headbutted my shin. I chose to take that as approval.

"Right then," I said. "Kev it is."

Within an hour, everyone knew his name. Within a day, it was like he'd always been called Kev.

I stood in the lounge, watching the residents call his name, and felt something shift inside me. Was it pride? Relief? I wasn't sure. But for the first time in months, I didn't feel like I was drowning. Kev had given us all something to hold onto—a name, a purpose, a reason to smile.

Residents started asking "Has Kev been in today?" or "When's Kev coming back?" as if he were a visiting professional rather than a stray cat who'd decided we were worth his time.

I ordered a name tag for him—a purple collar with a bell and a tag that read "Kev" on one side and "I live everywhere and nowhere. If found, I'm not lost," on the other, along with our phone number just in case.

The first time I tried to put it on him, Kev gave me a look of such profound betrayal that I nearly gave up. But I persisted, and eventually he accepted his new accessory with the resigned air of someone agreeing to wear a tie to a wedding.

"Looks smart," said Arthur when Kev made his rounds that afternoon, the little bell tinkling as he walked. "Very distinguished."

Kev jumped onto Arthur's lap—he was getting better at jumping, or perhaps just more confident about it—and settled in for a nap.

Arthur's gnarled hands, bent with arthritis, found their

way to Kev's fur and began the slow, gentle stroking that seemed to ease both of them.

I watched from the doorway, then pulled out my phone and took a photo. I'd started a file—just for records, I told myself, though really it was because I was already half in love with what was happening and wanted to remember it.

Later that evening, after Kev had departed for wherever he spent his nights, I found Maureen in the quiet lounge, staring out at the darkening garden.

"You alright, Maureen?"

She turned, and I was struck by how different she looked from a few weeks ago. Still sad—grief doesn't disappear—but less hollowed out. Less like a shell.

"I was just thinking," she said. "Harold would have liked Kev. He'd have pretended to be grumpy about him, said he was too scruffy, made a fuss. But I'd have caught him sneaking treats, giving him the best spot on the sofa."

"Kev has that effect on people," I said.

"It's funny," Maureen continued. "When I first came here, I thought my life was over. Everything good was behind me. But then this cat shows up, and suddenly I'm looking forward to something." She wiped her eyes. "Silly, isn't it? Getting emotional over a cat."

"It's not silly at all," I said quietly.

She smiled, a real smile, and turned back to the window. I left her there, silhouetted against the fading light, and went to do my evening rounds with a strange lightness in my chest.

Kev had been part of our lives for exactly two weeks, and already I couldn't imagine Rivermead without him.

***

In the weeks that followed, Kev became part of Rivermead's daily rhythm. I even started keeping what I half-jokingly called *The Good Book*—a spiral scrapbook with

Kev, the Care Home Cat

a rainbow on its cover where I recorded not the failures and problems, but the small victories - miracles - he seemed to create.

- The days when someone managed to feed themselves independently.
- The moment when two residents who'd never spoken before discovered a shared love of cricket.
- The first time someone smiled after weeks of depression.

Some were funny, some heartbreaking, all impossible to forget.

I didn't know it then, but I was documenting something important. Something that would matter more than I could possibly imagine.

By late February, Kev had established his schedule. The first hints of spring were in the air—soft sunlight, a faint sweetness from the daffodils pushing up by the gate, and the garden slowly waking from its winter slumber.

And then, as if on cue, most afternoons at two, Kev appeared, slipping through the gate with the quiet purpose that always seemed to follow him.

He arrived just after lunch had been cleared away and before afternoon activities began. He'd appear at the French windows in the dining room, mrow once, and wait to be let in with the patience of someone who knew his worth.

Most days, he preferred the lounge. He'd make his rounds, greeting each resident in turn—a headbutt here, a leg weave there, occasionally hopping onto a lap if the mood struck him. He had favourites, we noticed. Maureen, obviously. Arthur. A woman named Dorothy who'd been a librarian and still had that quiet, bookish calm that apparently appealed to cats.

Thursdays were different. Thursdays, Kev seemed to sense something about Thursdays.

That was the day Janet arrived.

She'd lived at home with her husband, Tom, until a series of incidents—leaving the cooker on, wandering off during the night, aggressive confusion—made it clear she needed round-the-clock care.

Tom visited nearly every day, sitting with her for hours, trying desperately to find the woman he'd married in the stranger who now sometimes couldn't remember his name.

It was heartbreaking in the way that only dementia can be: the long, slow goodbye while the person is still breathing.

Janet's first Thursday at Rivermead, she was agitated. She'd spent the morning asking for her mother (dead thirty years) and her hat (she didn't have one). She'd tried to leave three times, convinced she needed to get home to make dinner for children who were now middle-aged and living in other cities. Tom had visited at lunchtime, and the confusion of half-recognising him but not quite being sure had left them both in tears.

By two o'clock, Janet was pacing the corridor, wringing her hands, that particular dementia anxiety radiating off her in waves. Nothing we said or did seemed to help. She was lost somewhere in her own mind, and we couldn't find the map to bring her back.

Then Kev arrived.

He took one look at Janet, bypassed everyone else, and walked straight to her.

"Mrow," he said, very definitely.

Janet stopped pacing. She looked down.

"Oh," she said. "A cat."

Kev sat and began washing his face.

"We had a cat," Janet said to no one in particular. "When I was small. Called him... called him..." She frowned, reaching for a memory that slipped away like water. "Can't remember. But he was ginger. Like this one."

Kev finished washing, stood, and rubbed against her legs.

I held my breath. Unexpected touch could sometimes

trigger fear or aggression in residents with dementia. We'd been warned to approach Janet carefully, to announce ourselves, to move slowly.

But Kev wasn't following those rules, and somehow, it worked.

Janet bent down—carefully, her joints stiff—and touched Kev's head. He pushed up into her hand, purring.

"Soft," she said wonderingly. "He's very soft."

"That's Kev," I said gently. "He visits us when he feels like it."

"Kev," Janet repeated. Then, clearer: "Can I hold him?"

I looked at Kev. Kev looked at me. Then, deliberately, he jumped onto the chair next to Janet and waited.

She sat down, moving with the careful slowness of someone not quite sure of their own body, and Kev immediately stepped onto her lap.

The transformation was immediate. Janet's hands, which had been fluttering and anxious, settled on Kev's back. Her breathing slowed. The tight, frightened look around her eyes eased.

"Good boy," she murmured. "Good boy."

She sat like that for forty minutes, stroking Kev, occasionally talking to him in a soft voice about things that may or may not have been real—a house with a blue door, a garden with roses, a daughter's wedding. Kev stayed perfectly still, purring, solid and warm and real in a world that had become confusing and frightening.

When Tom arrived for his evening visit, he found his wife calm and smiling, a ginger cat on her lap.

"Tom," she said, and for once there was recognition in her voice. "Look. They have a cat here."

Tom's eyes met mine over her head. I saw gratitude there, and grief, and something else—maybe hope, maybe just relief that for this moment, this brief moment, she was okay.

"I can see that," he said, sitting down next to her. "Hello, cat."

"His name's Kev," Janet informed him, in the same tone she might use to introduce a visiting dignitary.

"Hello, Kev," Tom corrected himself.

Kev mrowed but didn't move, content to be the bridge between past and present, between confusion and clarity, for as long as he was needed.

* * *

In the weeks that followed, I kept writing in The Good Book — a record of what Kev did, who he helped, and how.

"He's got better attendance than some of our staff," Denise joked one morning, though there was truth underneath the humour.

"He's more reliable than most people," I agreed, watching him through the window sniffing at daffodils. "Takes his job seriously."

And he did. Every day at two and other times too when he felt like it.

Reading back through the Good Book now, I can see how his visits deepened. What began as distraction turned into something quieter, heavier, almost sacred. One story still stops me every time I think of it—George's.

George didn't speak.

George had arrived in January, after a massive stroke left him with locked-in syndrome—fully conscious, fully aware, but unable to move anything except his eyes. His wife, Patricia, visited daily, talking to him for hours, reading the newspaper aloud, describing the world he could no longer interact with.

It was heartbreaking to watch. George's eyes would track her movements, clearly understanding, clearly there, but trapped in a body that no longer obeyed him.

The staff did their best, but there's only so much you can do for someone who can't communicate their needs beyond yes-or-no eye blinks. One blink for yes, two for no. A tediously slow way to navigate the world.

Kev met George on a cold grey Friday in February.

He walked into George's room during his rounds and stopped short when he saw the man in the specialised bed, eyes open but body still.

I was checking George's fluid charts and held my breath. Sometimes residents who couldn't move would be frightened by unexpected approaches, and George couldn't even flinch away.

But Kev didn't approach the bed. Instead, he jumped onto the windowsill where George could see him without straining, and sat down. Just sat, tail wrapped around his paws, looking back at George.

George's eyes focused on the cat. One slow blink.

Kev mrowed softly, as if in greeting.

I watched, fascinated, as they stared at each other. It should have been awkward—this one-sided interaction—but somehow it wasn't. There was a communication happening that I couldn't quite define.

After several minutes, Kev jumped down and walked to the bed. He paused, looked at me as if asking permission, then very carefully climbed onto the bed beside George. Not on him—George's body was too fragile for that—but beside, close enough that George could see him clearly.

Kev settled down, purring audibly. George's eyes moved to watch him, and I swear I saw something shift in his expression. Not quite a smile—he couldn't manage that—but a softening. A lessening of the terrible isolation.

"Would you like Kev to stay with you for a bit?" I asked George.

One blink. Yes.

"I'll be back in twenty minutes to check on you both."

One blink.

I left them there, man and cat, both silent but somehow

communicating in a language that transcended words.

When Patricia arrived that afternoon, she found George with Kev still beside him. The cat had barely moved, content to be a warm, purring presence.

"Oh," Patricia said, her hand flying to her mouth. "Oh, George, you've made a friend."

One blink.

She sat in her usual chair and began her usual routine of reading the newspaper, but something had changed. The room felt less heavy. Less like a prison.

The room was quiet except for the hum of the oxygen machine, the rustle of newspaper pages, and Kev's purr thrumming like a small engine. Outside, rain tapped against the window in a rhythm that made the room feel even more contained, even more intimate.

Afterwards, walking Patricia out, she gripped my arm. "Thank you for letting the cat stay with him. George gets so lonely. I can see it in his eyes—the loneliness is worse than the paralysis sometimes. But today, just for a bit, he had company that didn't feel like duty."

"Kev seems to like him."

"It's more than that." She wiped her eyes. "George always loved animals. We had to rehome our dog when he came here—nobody to care for it, and I just couldn't manage on my own. I think he grieved that as much as anything. It broke my heart too. But now…"

From that day forward, Kev always spent time with George on his visits. They developed their own routine: Kev would arrive, greet George, settle beside him, and purr. George would watch him, one-blink conversations about nothing and everything.

Sometimes, Patricia would read to both of them. Sometimes the room would just be quiet except for Kev's purring—that deep, rhythmic sound that seemed to say *you're not alone, I'm here, it's okay.*

One day I arrived to find Patricia in tears beside George's bed, Kev between them.

"He blinked it out," she sobbed. "Letter by letter, it took forty minutes, but he spelled out: 'Lucky. Cat. Understand.'"

She looked at me with streaming eyes. "The cat understands. That's what he wanted to tell me. That the cat understands what it's like to be trapped, to be looked past, to be waiting for someone to really see you."

I had to leave the room. Had to stand in the corridor with my hand over my mouth, fighting back tears.

Because George was right. Kev did understand. Maybe because he'd been a stray—overlooked, underestimated, surviving on the margins. Or maybe because cats are just better at seeing the essential parts of people, the parts that matter when everything else is stripped away.

George lived another three months. Towards the end, when even blinking became difficult, Kev would still visit. Would still settle beside him, purring steadily, a warm point of contact in the gathering dark.

When George died, Kev was there. We sat with George as his breathing slowed, became irregular, finally stopped.

Kev, who'd been on the bed the whole time, stood up. He touched his nose to George's hand—the hand that hadn't moved in months—and mrowed once, softly.

Then he jumped down and left the room.

"He knew," Patricia whispered. "He knew George was gone."

Later, I added to the Good Book:

George died peacefully in the early hours of this morning, Patricia and Kev with him. Kev seems to make a point of coming outside his normal time just when he knows he's needed.

I've been thinking about the friendship they had—how it existed almost entirely in silence, in presence, in the simple act of being together.

> *Sometimes I think we talk too much, try too hard to fill the quiet with words and explanations. Kev knows better. He knows that sometimes the greatest gift is just staying. Just being there. Not fixing, not explaining, just witnessing. Just caring enough to sit beside someone in their darkness until the light comes back. Or, in George's case, until the darkness becomes permanent, and then sitting a bit longer, seeing them off.*
>
> *Rest well, George. I hope wherever you are now, you can move again, speak again, dance again. And I hope there are cats.*

I didn't tell anyone this, but that night I went home and cried for an hour. Not just for George—though I'd grown fond of him in those months—but for the sheer impossibility of what we do. We care for people knowing they'll die. We form attachments knowing they'll end. We love temporary things with our whole hearts.

And Kev does it too. He loves them and loses them and comes back anyway, Day after Day. And the odd times in between.

Denise, wiping her eyes, muttered that Kev was probably charging George for therapy sessions in catnip.

After George's funeral, Rivermead felt changed. Softer somehow. People spoke in lower voices for a few days, as if afraid to disturb the space he'd left behind. Kev carried on, padding through the corridors like a priest after a service, reminding us that life went on.

* * *

Eleanor arrived at Rivermead on a bright February morning wearing pearls, perfectly applied pink lipstick, and an expression that dared anyone to suggest she was old.

She swept through the entrance like visiting royalty, her daughter Caroline trailing behind with an overnight bag and the air of someone who hadn't slept properly in months.

Kev, the Care Home Cat

"Just for a week or two," Eleanor announced to the reception area, though no one had asked. "While my house is being redecorated. I'm perfectly capable of managing on my own, but Caroline insists."

Caroline caught my eye with a look that said: *Please play along.*

I extended my hand. "Mrs. Hartley, welcome to Rivermead. I'm Dawn Milsom, the manager. Let me show you to your room."

"It's temporary," Eleanor repeated, as if saying it enough times would make it true.

Her "room" was actually one of our nicest suites—ground floor, bay windows overlooking the garden, enough space for a few pieces of the antique furniture Caroline had insisted on bringing. Eleanor inspected the room with the thoroughness of a health inspector, running one finger along the windowsill to check for dust.

"It'll do," she said finally. "For a short stay."

After we'd settled her in, Caroline pulled me aside in the corridor. Her hands were shaking slightly.

"She thinks this is a hotel," Caroline said in a rush. "Or a guest house. She doesn't understand—or won't accept—that this is permanent. The doctors said it's better not to push it right now. Let her adjust gradually."

"How advanced is the dementia?"

"Early to moderate. She still knows who I am, mostly. But she gets confused about time. Thinks her mother is still alive. And she's been talking about her cat constantly—Tibbles. He died in 1998, but yesterday she insisted I needed to go and feed him."

I nodded, having heard similar stories countless times. "We'll follow her lead. If she wants to believe this is temporary, that's fine for now."

"Thank you." Caroline's relief was palpable. "I just... I couldn't do it anymore. She nearly set the kitchen on fire last week trying to make tea. And she keeps going out in the middle of the night looking for things that don't exist. I have two children, a job, a husband who works nights..." She broke off, crying quietly. "I'm a terrible daughter."

"You're an exhausted daughter who's doing her best. That's different."

Over the next few days, Eleanor maintained her fiction with impressive commitment. She praised certain aspects of the "hotel" (the daffodils in the garden, the afternoon tea service) and criticised others (the tea was "stewed," the television in the lounge too loud). She told anyone who would listen that she was leaving just as soon as her decorator finished, and her cat was probably beside himself without her.

The other residents played along beautifully. When Eleanor complained about the 'other guests' to Maureen, Maureen simply agreed that yes, some people were rather noisy, weren't they?

"She's scared," Denise told me quietly afterward. "You can see it underneath all that bluster. She's terrified of what's happening to her."

It was the following afternoon when Eleanor met Kev.

I was in the lounge doing medication rounds when he arrived, padding across the carpet with his usual self-assurance, tail held high. Several residents called out greetings. Kev acknowledged them with regal nods but kept walking, apparently on a mission.

Eleanor was sitting in the bay window, reading a gardening magazine. Or pretending to read—I'd noticed the same page had been in front of her for twenty minutes.

And then she saw him.

Her magazine fell from her hands. Her face transformed —every line of carefully maintained composure crumbling in an instant.

"Tibbles!" The word came out as a gasp, half-joy, half-sob. "Tibbles, you came back!"

Before anyone could explain, before I could even move, Eleanor was on her knees on the carpet—no small feat for an eighty-two-year-old woman—arms outstretched.

Kev walked straight into them.

He didn't pause or sniff or do his usual cat assessment. He just walked directly into Eleanor's embrace and nestled against her chest, purring with that deep, rolling purr that seemed to come from his very core.

"Oh my clever, clever boy," Eleanor whispered into his fur, rocking slightly. "You found me. I knew you would. You never did like being left behind, did you?"

I felt the air change in the room. Staff stopped what they were doing. Other residents turned to watch. Even Bert, who was usually oblivious to anything that didn't involve his newspaper, looked up with something like wonder on his face.

"Someone should tell her," Denise whispered beside me. "That it's not her cat."

"No," I said quietly. "Not yet."

Because what was happening was bigger than facts. Eleanor's hands, which had been trembling with anxiety since she arrived, were steady now as they stroked Kev's head. Her breathing, which had been quick and shallow, had slowed to match his purring. And her face—her carefully made-up, determinedly cheerful face—had finally relaxed into something genuine.

She wasn't pretending anymore. She was just... herself.

After a few minutes, Eleanor gently scooped Kev up and carried him to her chair by the window. He settled onto her lap like he'd always belonged there, a perfect orange circle of contentment.

"You've gotten scruffy," Eleanor told him, adjusting his collar. "We'll need to brush you properly. And your ear—what happened to your ear? Have you been fighting again?"

Kev mrowed softly, as if confirming this.

"I thought so. You never could resist a scrap." She stroked the damaged ear tenderly. "But you're home now. That's what matters."

I started to approach, to gently explain, but Denise caught my arm. "Leave them," she mouthed.

So I did. We all did. We watched Eleanor talk to Kev for the next hour, her voice gaining strength with every sentence, colour returning to her cheeks.

She told him about the house she was leaving (though it had been sold three months ago). About the decorator who was taking forever (there was no decorator). About how she'd missed him terribly and was so glad he'd found her.

Kev listened to it all with perfect patience, purring steadily, occasionally butting his head against her hand when she stopped stroking.

When Caroline arrived for her evening visit, she stopped dead in the doorway.

"Is that...?"

"That's Kev," I said quietly. "Our therapy cat."

"But Mum thinks—"

"I know."

We watched Eleanor show Kev to Caroline, explaining in the patient tone people use with children that yes, this was Tibbles, and wasn't it clever of him to find the hotel she was staying in?

Caroline looked at me helplessly. "Should I correct her?"

"What would that accomplish?"

She thought about it, then shook her head. "Nothing. Nothing good, anyway."

From that day forward, Eleanor and Kev were inseparable whenever he visited. She'd wait for him just before two, dressed in her best, pearls on, lipstick perfect. The fiction that she was temporarily staying at a hotel had quietly disappeared. She now simply lived here, in this place where her cat could visit her.

She started taking out her photograph albums—beautiful old leather ones with tissue paper between the pages—and narrating her life to Kev as if he'd lived it alongside her.

"Here's when you stole the roast chicken straight off the counter," she'd say, pointing to a Christmas photo from the 1970s. "Don't think I've forgotten. I had to serve ham that year instead. And here—" she turned the page carefully, "—here's your favourite chair by the fire. I had to reupholster it twice because of your claws."

Kev would sit beside her, watching the pages turn, tail flicking occasionally as if he remembered these things too.

The residents learned to play along. When Eleanor mentioned Tibbles, they'd nod and smile and ask how he was. Even Bert, crusty Bert, would inquire after "the cat" when Eleanor passed his table at lunch.

"How's Tibbles today, then?"

"Very well, thank you. A bit greedy at breakfast, but that's cats for you."

"That's cats indeed."

One day, about a month after Eleanor's arrival, she showed Kev a photograph I'd never seen before. Black and white, faded, showing a much younger Eleanor—perhaps forty—standing in a garden with a ginger cat in her arms.

"That's really you," she said softly to Kev. "That's us, before everything got so complicated. You were just a kitten then. Look how small you were."

She traced the cat in the photo with one finger. "Robert had just died—that's your Uncle Robert. He hated cats, but you made him sneeze on purpose, didn't you?" Kev blinked as if agreeing. Her voice caught. "After he died, you were all I had for a while. Just you and me in that big house."

Kev pushed his head against her hand.

"I'm glad you found me here," Eleanor continued. "I was afraid you wouldn't. Afraid you'd forget me, the way I forget things now. But you remembered. Cats always remember, don't they?"

I was standing in the doorway, and I had to turn away, tears streaming down my face. Because she was right, in a way. Kev had remembered something—not her specifically, but what she needed. And he'd given it to her.

That afternoon, I made an entry in The Good Book:

Eleanor called Kev "Tibbles" today and for an hour remembered her life clearly—not as it is, but as it was. As it should have been. She showed him photographs and told him stories, and whether any of it was literally true doesn't matter. What matters is that for that hour, she wasn't confused or scared. She was exactly who she used to be: a woman with a past, a history, a cat who loved her.

Maybe memory lives not just in the mind but in the warmth of something purring on your knee. Maybe truth isn't always about facts. Maybe sometimes it's about finding comfort in whatever form it takes.

From that day, Eleanor kept her photo album by her chair. When Kev visited, she'd pat the cushion beside her. "Come on, Tibbles. Time to look at our memories."

And somehow, for as long as Kev sat with her, she did remember—not perfectly, not accurately, but deeply. Snatches of faces, places, moments long buried emerged in fragments. Her husband, who she still sometimes forgot was dead. Her daughter Caroline's wedding, though she'd call Caroline by the wrong name. The house with the blue door that may or may not have been real.

Caroline came one afternoon and found them like that—her mother and a cat that wasn't Tibbles, looking at photographs together. Her face softened in a way I hadn't seen before.

"She hasn't told those stories in years," she whispered to me. "She doesn't even remember my wedding day and her grandchildren most days. But she remembered the cat."

Kev, the Care Home Cat

"Memory is strange," I said. "It hides in unexpected places."

"He's helping her, isn't he? Not just making her happy—actually helping her hold onto things."

"I think so. Though I couldn't tell you how or why."

Later, when Eleanor nodded off with Kev still on her lap, Caroline knelt beside the chair and stroked the cat's head.

"Thank you," she murmured, so quietly I almost didn't hear. "Thank you for bringing her home for a bit. Even if it's not the home that exists anymore. Even if it's just in her head. Thank you."

Kev opened one eye, gave Caroline that slow blink of acknowledgment, then went back to his vigil.

That night I wrote in The Good Book:

Sometimes memory hides until it feels safe. Today a scruffy ginger cat made it safe again. Eleanor for an hour remembered everyone she'd loved—husband, home, the life before everything started slipping away.

Maybe memory isn't stored in the brain at all. Maybe it lives in touch, in scent, in the steady rhythm of a purr. Maybe it's less about neural pathways and more about feeling safe enough to remember.

Eleanor lived at Rivermead for another two years. She never stopped calling Kev "Tibbles," and we never corrected her. Why would we? In all the ways that mattered, he was her Tibbles. He was exactly the cat she needed him to be.

***

Rain streaked the garden windows. March rain—the miserable kind that's not quite cold enough to be snow, but just enough to make everything damp and grey. But through the window, if you looked carefully, you could see the very first tulips pushing through mulch outside as Kev patrolled his new domain.

Not everyone was instantly charmed by Kev.

Bert in room six made his position clear from day one: "I don't like cats. Never have. Dogs are loyal. Cats are selfish little bastards who only care about themselves."

"Noted," I said, making a mental note to keep Kev away from Bert's room.

Bert was eighty-seven, ex-army, and carried himself like he was still on parade even when shuffling with a walker. The faint creak of the walker's wheels on the linoleum floor were familiar sounds in the corridors of Rivermead.

He'd lost his wife five years ago and both his sons now lived abroad—one in Australia, one in Canada. Christmas cards arrived annually. Phone calls were sporadic. Bert covered his loneliness with irascibility and strict routines.

Breakfast at 7:30 sharp. Newspaper at 8:00 (Telegraph, not the Mail, don't get them confused). Coffee at 10:30. Lunch at 1.00. Afternoon nap. Tea at 3:00. Dinner at 6:00. Bed at 9:00. Any deviation was met with complaints.

Kev, naturally, made it his mission to win Bert over.

The first time, Kev simply sat outside Bert's room and stared at the closed door.

"He's not interested," I told the cat. "Some people just don't like cats. It's fine. Plenty of other residents want your attention."

Kev ignored me and continued staring.

The second time, Bert's door was open—Claire, our care assistant helping him with something—and Kev slipped inside.

"Oi! Get that thing out of here!" Bert's voice carried down the corridor.

I rushed in to find Kev sitting on Bert's bed, examining the collection of military photographs on the bedside table with apparent interest.

"Sorry, Bert. Come on, Kev, out."

"Bloody cat. Probably covered in fleas."

"He's not, actually. He is very clean." I scooped up Kev,

who mrowed his protest. "I'll make sure he doesn't bother you again."

"See that you do."

The third time, I wasn't there to witness it, but Denise told me about it later, laughing so hard she could barely speak.

"So Bert's in the lounge, yeah? Having his morning coffee, reading his paper. And Kev just... walks over, jumps on the arm of the chair, and sits down. Doesn't try to get on his lap or anything, just sits next to him. And Bert ignores him completely. Just keeps reading his paper like there's not a cat two inches away."

"And?"

"And nothing! They sat like that for twenty minutes! Bert reading, Kev watching him read. Then Kev got bored and left. But here's the thing—when Kev left, I saw Bert watching him go. Not annoyed. Not irritated. Just... watching."

"Interesting."

"Very interesting. I reckon Kev knows something we don't."

A week later, I was doing my rounds when I heard something unusual coming from Bert's room. Laughter.

I stopped outside the door, which was slightly ajar. Inside, Bert was sitting in his chair by the window, Kev on his lap, while Bert read aloud from his newspaper.

"*'Council plans new traffic scheme for town centre',*" Bert read in his gruff voice. *"'Local businesses express concern about loss of parking.'* Load of nonsense, of course. They've been banging on about that bypass for thirty years, never happens."

Kev mrowed.

"Exactly!" Bert said. "You get it. More than most people around here."

He turned the page, one hand absently stroking Kev's back. "Right, what's next? *'Royal family make official visit to...'*

Oh, who cares. Let's find the sports section."

I backed away quietly, not wanting to break the spell.

Later, when Kev was making his way out for the day, I caught up with Bert in the corridor.

"Lovely afternoon," I said carefully.

"Hmph."

"Kev seemed to enjoy spending time with you."

"Did he?"

"He did. In fact, I'd say he's quite taken with you."

Bert looked at me, his expression unreadable. Then, grudgingly: "He's not as stupid as most cats."

"High praise."

"Don't get any ideas. I still don't like cats."

"Of course not."

"But if that particular cat wants to visit sometimes... well. I suppose it's not a complete nuisance."

"I'll let him know."

After that, mornings became Bert's time. Kev would arrive, make a cursory tour of the other residents, then head straight to Bert's room where the door would be—accidentally, Bert claimed—slightly open. They'd spend an hour together, Bert reading aloud from his paper, telling Kev stories about his army days, occasionally grumbling about the state of the world while Kev listened with what appeared to be great interest.

"You know why he likes me?" Bert asked one day when I brought tea to his room. Kev was asleep on his lap, a ginger puddle of contentment.

"Why's that?"

"I don't baby him. Don't talk to him in that stupid voice people use with animals. Just talk to him normal, like he's got a brain. Which he does. He appreciates that."

"I'm sure he does."

"And I don't make a fuss. He comes when he wants, leaves when he wants. No expectations. That's how it should be."

I looked at Bert's hand, still absently stroking Kev's fur, and thought about loneliness. About sons on the other side of the world. About how sometimes the smallest connection —a cat who chooses to sit with you, not because he has to, but because he wants to—can matter more than grand gestures.

"You're probably right," I said.

"Course I'm right. Been right about most things for eighty-seven years."

Kev opened one eye, looked at me, then went back to sleep.

I left them there, Bert and Kev, the refusenik and the cat, neither admitting how much they'd come to need these mornings.

Watching Bert stroke his fur, something unknotted in me too. Maybe it wasn't just the residents who needed rescuing. Maybe I did as well, though I wouldn't have admitted it then.

* * *

Spring had fully arrived by the time I admitted to myself that I was lonely.

Not lonely for company—I had that in abundance. Residents, staff, family members visiting, the endless parade of people that is a care home's daily life. But lonely for something else. For someone who wasn't my responsibility. Someone I could be vulnerable with. Someone who chose me, specifically, not because I was the manager or the person who solved problems, but just... me.

Denise had been hinting at it for months. "When was the last time you went on a date?" she'd ask, casual as anything, while we did medication rounds or sorted through paperwork.

"I don't have time for dating."

"Everyone has time for dating. You just have to make it a priority."

But making it a priority felt impossible when work consumed everything. When I went home too tired to do more than heat up something frozen and fall asleep in front of Netflix. When the thought of small talk and forced smiles with a stranger felt more exhausting than any shift at Rivermead.

Then Kev started his matchmaking side hustle, and suddenly I didn't have a choice.

***

By the time Bert and Kev reached their uneasy truce, the cat had worked his way into every corner of Rivermead.

What I didn't expect was how quietly he'd started working on me, too—nudging, in his own feline way, at the parts of my life that had nothing to do with care plans or residents.

By then, Kev had fixed more hearts than any therapist I'd ever met and I suppose I started to wonder if a little of his luck might rub off on me. I wasn't looking for grand romance—just proof that I could still connect with someone whose idea of a night out didn't involve a hoist or a blood-pressure cuff.

It started, as these things often do, with wine and Denise.

"You're thirty-six," she declared over staff-room prosecco one Friday night. "You can't keep spending your evenings doing risk assessments and watching *Bake Off* repeats. You need to meet someone."

"I meet people all the time," I protested. "Usually they're over eighty and complain about the custard."

"You've got compassion fatigue," she said, handing me her phone. "You need someone who isn't incontinent or ninety."

Denise rolled her eyes as she pointed at the screen. "Get

Kev, the Care Home Cat

on this dating app. It's alright."

I signed up to the free dating app purely to shut her up. Rain drummed on the flat roof above us—March rain, harsh and loud as I started scrolling through possibilities.

I stared at the screen. "He's holding a fish."

"Automatic left," said Denise.

Within minutes I was knee-deep in profiles: men posing with cars (they probably didn't own), men holding fish, men listing "banter' — or worse "bants" — as a personality trait. I was about to delete the app when Kev jumped onto the sofa and planted his paw squarely on my phone. Swipe left.

"You're right," I told him. "Anyone quoting 'work hard, play hard' deserves to be single."

Denise burst out laughing. "The cat's your matchmaker now!" She wiped laughter tears from her eyes. "Could do worse, mind!" she said with a straight face before corpsing into more laughter.

But as the giggles settled, I caught Kev's steady gaze, and it hit me—he'd taught me to trust my instincts again.

Later in the staffroom, curiosity got the better of me. I sat on the sofa, app open again on my phone, Kev purring beside me.

"Alright," I told him. "We'll give this a go. One meow for yes, silence for no."

The first man had a mirror selfie and a description that said *'Gym, gin, and sin.'* Kev turned his back immediately.

The second was smiling with a dog. Kev leaned forward, sniffed the screen, then nudged my hand decisively right.

"You approve?"

"Mrow."

I swiped.

It became our breaktime ritual. I'd sit with tea, Kev draped over my knees like an orange blanket, and we'd assess my options, me scrolling, him judging. He was uncannily accurate: everyone he approved of turned out

39

kind or funny in their messages; everyone he rejected inevitably revealed themselves to be arrogant or dull.

Good Book: informal note: Staff morale improved by 100% after discovery that Kev can spot red flags faster than HR.

Denise started calling it *The Kev Algorithm.*

I wasn't sure whether I was lonely or just curious, but for the first time in years I felt... hopeful.

Claire caught me swiping one night during a late paperwork session. "What are you doing?"

"Therapy," I said. "Experimental programme in animal-assisted matchmaking."

She peered at the screen. "He's fit."

"Kev doesn't think so," I said as the cat yawned and turned his back.

After too much swiping and not enough matching, Denise decided my "research phase" had gone on too long.

"You're not running a cat-approved PhD," she said, watching me scroll through yet another profile while Kev dozed on my lap. "You're supposed to meet an actual human being. In person. With your actual face."

"I am meeting people."

"You're collecting data. There's a difference."

She had a point. For three weeks, I'd been using Kev as an excuse to avoid actual dates. His approval process was thorough, after all. Very thorough. Why rush things?

"One proper date," Denise insisted. "This weekend. No backing out. The cat can vet them afterwards if your match makes it past round one."

So I did it. I agreed to meet a fellow called Martin on Saturday for lunch.

He taught economics and spoke as if life was a spreadsheet. His profile mentioned hill walking, craft beer, and "intelligent conversation." His photo showed a man in his early forties with a neat beard and a smile that didn't quite reach his eyes.

Kev had been ambivalent about his profile—no hissing, but no enthusiasm either. A cautious approval, I'd interpreted. Worth meeting.

I should have trusted the lack of enthusiasm.

Martin arrived at the café exactly on time, wearing a shirt so precisely ironed it could have drawn blood. He ordered sparkling water with a slice of lime—not lemon, lime, very important distinction—and spent the first ten minutes explaining his morning workout routine in granular detail.

"I track everything," he said, pulling out his phone to show me an app with more graphs than my Year 10 maths textbook. "Heart rate, calories burned, optimal recovery time. Data-driven fitness is the only way to see real results."

"Right," I said, watching my coffee grow cold.

"You should try it. I could set you up with a programme. Nothing too intense to start—just tracking your steps, caloric intake, basic metrics."

"I work twelve-hour shifts in a care home. I probably hit my step count by lunchtime."

"But do you track it? Because if you're not measuring, you're not improving."

He said this with the earnest intensity of someone who'd never considered that not everything worth doing could be quantified on a spreadsheet.

Lunch didn't improve. He told me about his ISA share portfolio (diversified), his meal prep routine (optimised), and his opinion on mortgage rates (strong). When I tried to talk about my work, he nodded politely but his eyes glazed over.

"Care work must be quite... repetitive," he said. "I imagine the intellectual stimulation is limited."

I set down my fork carefully. "Repetitive?"

"I just mean—it's physical work, isn't it? Bathing, feeding, that sort of thing. Not much problem-solving involved."

"Right. Except for managing medication interactions for twenty residents with different conditions, handling complex family dynamics, navigating dementia care protocols, dealing with end-of-life decisions, maintaining safeguarding standards, managing staff, meeting CQC requirements, and occasionally preventing people from dying. But yes, apart from that, very little problem-solving."

He blinked. "I didn't mean—"

"I need to get back," I said, already reaching for my bag. "Early shift tomorrow."

"But it's Saturday."

"Care homes don't close on weekends."

I left him with the bill—petty, perhaps, but satisfying—and drove home with my hands gripping the steering wheel too tightly.

Back at the Home, Kev was waiting in my office, sprawled across the desk as if he'd been expecting me. It was as if he'd come in especially at the weekend just to say 'I told you so'.

"You were right," I told him. "The lukewarm approval should have been a red flag."

He blinked slowly, that particular combination of sympathy and superiority that only cats can achieve.

"Next time, I'm trusting the hiss."

I watched Kev curl up beside me, a quiet reminder that some connections are worth waiting for.

***

The second disaster came two weeks later with Sam, a graphic designer with kind eyes and a profile full of artsy photos. Kev had given cautious approval—a head tilt, a considering mrow, nothing definitive.

Again, I should have waited for enthusiasm.

We met at a wine bar in town. Sam was charming for the first fifteen minutes—funny stories about difficult clients, questions about my work that seemed as if he was genuinely interested. I started to relax, started to think maybe this one would be different.

Then he ordered a second glass of wine and said: "So, I have to tell you about something important to me."

"Okay."

"I'm really passionate about water fluoridation."

"Sorry?"

"The government putting fluoride in water. It's a massive conspiracy. They're literally poisoning us."

I stared at him. "Fluoride. In the water."

"I know it sounds crazy, but hear me out." He pulled up a website on his phone—lots of red text, exclamation points, a suspicious number of Comic Sans headers. "See? They claim it's for dental health, but it's actually about population control. Makes people docile, easier to manipulate."

"Sam, fluoride in water is a well-established public health measure. The evidence—"

He tapped his forehead. "That's what they want you to think. The studies are all funded by Big Pharma."

He went on for twenty minutes. Toxins. Government control. The importance of filtering all your water. Did I know my shower was poisoning me? Because he had a great recommendation for filters.

I excused myself after dessert, claiming an early shift. Again.

In the car, I called Denise. "He seemed so normal," I said.

"They always do at first. That's how they get you."

"Kev tried to warn me. He wasn't enthusiastic."

"The cat knows. You need to stop ignoring the cat."

Back in the staff room, Kev was sprawled across the desk. Again waiting to tell me so. He blinked slowly, that long, silent judgement cats do better than any human.

"You were right," I told him.

He yawned without mercy.

It wasn't funny, really; it was that dull ache of trying and failing again.

That evening, Kev was stretched out lazily on my desk, his eyes barely open. When I sat down, he stood, stretched elaborately, and walked across my keyboard—managing to close the dating site window in the process.

"Subtle," I said.

He jumped into my lap, turned three times, and settled with the air of someone making a point.

"You're right," I admitted, stroking his head. "I'm trying too hard. Forcing things with people you're not sure about because I'm lonely. That's not healthy, is it?"

He purred, which I chose to interpret as agreement.

"So what do I do? Just wait for someone you actually like? That could take years."

Kev opened one eye, gave me a look that clearly said *and?*, then went back to sleep.

I sat there for a long time, this cat purring on my lap, and thought about what Denise had said about data collection. Maybe that's what I'd been doing—treating dating like a care plan that needed optimising, when what I actually needed was to trust my instincts. And Kev's instincts, which had proven significantly better than mine.

I wrote in the Good Book:

Two dates, two disasters.

One man who treated life like a spreadsheet, one who thought the government was poisoning him through tap water. Kev's lukewarm approvals should have been my warning.

Note to self: when the cat isn't enthusiastic, walk away. He's never wrong about people. He sees something I'm too hopeful—or too desperate—to see.

Also note: loneliness isn't solved by accepting less than I deserve. Better to be alone and whole than partnered and diminished. The right person will make Kev purr immediately, not after careful consideration.

Trust the cat. Always trust the cat.

The next morning, Maureen asked how my "courting" was going.

"Badly," I admitted.

"What does Kev think?"

"He thinks I should have higher standards."

She laughed. "Smart cat. You should listen to him. My Harold—he knew within five minutes if I'd like someone. Had an instinct for character. Kev's the same. If he doesn't immediately warm to someone, there's a reason."

"So I should just... wait?"

"You should trust yourself. And your ginger colleague." She smiled. "The right person will just fit. You'll know because Kev will know, and he won't be subtle about it."

She was right, of course. They were all right. But knowing that didn't make the waiting any easier, or the loneliness any less sharp on quiet evenings alone with my ready meal in my empty flat.

"High standards from now on," I told him. "No more lukewarm approvals."

Kev, watching from the sofa, gave an approving mrow.

If the right person existed, Kev would know them when he saw them. And until then, I'd wait. Because settling for Martin or Sam or anyone else the cat wasn't sure about would be worse than being alone.

At least, that's what I told myself as I heated up another ready meal for one and tried not to think about how quiet my flat was.

* * *

He seemed different. Michael.

His profile was sparse but genuine—no gym selfies, no fish, no quotes about hustling. Just one photo: him at a bookshop, slight smile, kind eyes. His description mentioned his rescue terrier and a fondness for history podcasts.

When I read it aloud to Kev, he'd done something unusual—stood up, walked closer to the phone, and stared at Michael's photo for a solid ten seconds before giving a single, decisive mrow.

"That's a yes?"

Another mrow. Definite.

"Alright then. Let's hope you're right."

We'd messaged for three days before arranging to meet. Proper conversation, not the usual stilted small talk. He'd made me laugh—actually laugh—with a story about his terrier eating an entire Victoria sponge off the counter. When I told him about Kev's matchmaking services, he'd replied: *Smart cat. I'd like to meet him sometime.*

The night before we were supposed to meet, I barely slept. Ridiculous at thirty-six to feel like a teenager, but there it was—butterflies and anxiety and hope all tangled together in my chest.

We'd arranged to meet at a café in town. Neutral territory, easy escape routes if needed. I arrived five minutes early, ordered tea I didn't drink, and tried not to check my phone every thirty seconds.

Michael arrived exactly on time. He looked like his photo but more so—the kind eyes, the slight uncertainty in his smile as he spotted me.

"Dawn?"

"Michael. Hi."

"Sorry, is this weird? Meeting someone from an app feels inherently weird."

"Deeply weird," I agreed, and felt myself relax slightly. "But we're both here, so we might as well commit to the weirdness."

He laughed—a genuine laugh that crinkled his eyes—and sat down across from me.

The first ten minutes were lovely. We fell into conversation easily, that rare synchronicity where you're not

Kev, the Care Home Cat

performing or second-guessing, just talking. He asked about work with actual interest, didn't flinch when I mentioned dementia care, even shared that his gran had Alzheimer's before she died.

"It was hard," he said. "Watching her forget us. But the care home she was in—they were good to her. Made her last years bearable."

"That's what we try to do."

"I can tell. You light up when you talk about your residents. And this cat—Kev? He sounds remarkable."

"He is. He's—"

Michael's phone rang.

He glanced at it, frowned slightly. "Sorry, I should take this. It's my brother. Won't be a second."

"Of course."

He stepped outside. I watched through the window as he answered, his expression shifting from neutral to concerned to something harder to read. The call lasted maybe two minutes. Then he lowered the phone, stood there for a moment looking at nothing in particular, and walked away.

Just walked away.

I sat there, cup halfway to my lips, brain struggling to process what had just happened. He'd left. Actually left. Mid-date, mid-conversation, mid-everything.

I waited five minutes, thinking maybe he'd gone to his car, or needed air, or—

Ten minutes.

Fifteen.

The waitress came over, that careful sympathy on her face that said she'd seen this before. "Can I get you anything else, love?"

"No. Thank you. Just the bill."

"Are you alright?"

Was I? I genuinely didn't know. I felt weirdly detached, like watching myself in a film where the protagonist makes terrible dating choices.

"I think," I said slowly, "I've just been ghosted in real time."

"Happens more than you'd think." She brought me a napkin along with the bill. "One time, I had a woman whose date climbed out the toilet window. At least yours left through the front door."

I laughed—a slightly unhinged sound—and paid for my tea and his untouched coffee.

The drive back to Rivermead was a blur. I kept checking my phone at red lights, convinced there'd be a message explaining everything. Emergency. Misunderstanding. Dead battery. Something that made sense.

Nothing.

By the time I pulled into the car park, the shock had worn off and rage had taken its place. Not just at Michael—though there was plenty of that—but at myself. For hoping. For letting Kev convince me this one might be different. For spending last night imagining what it might be like to actually connect with someone.

Denise found me in the staff room ten minutes later, still in my good coat, staring at the wall. She was, as always, running on caffeine and mischief, her eyes sharp despite the long hours.

"That was quick. Was he that bad?"

"He left."

"What?"

"Halfway through. Got a phone call, stepped outside, never came back."

Denise's face went through several expressions—disbelief, anger, something that might have been murderous intent. "He just... walked away?"

"Yep."

"Without saying anything?"

"Not a word."

"That absolute—" She used a word that would have made Bert proud. "Right. We're going to find him and I'm going to—"

"Denise. It's fine."

"It's not fine. It's the opposite of fine."

"I know. But what am I supposed to do? Hunt him down and demand an explanation? He clearly didn't want to be there. At least he showed me that quickly rather than wasting more of my time."

"You're being very calm about this."

"I'm not calm. I'm furious. But I'm also at work, and we have residents who need me, and I can't fall apart over some man I talked to for ten minutes."

That was the theory, anyway. In practice, I made it another hour before the calm cracked.

I was helping Grace with her afternoon tea when she asked, casually, "How was your date?"

And just like that, I started crying. Not gentle tears—ugly, gulping sobs that I couldn't control or stop.

Grace looked alarmed. "Oh. Oh no. Was he... did he... fuck, I don't have... words for..."

"He left," I managed between sobs. "Just walked out."

"What a... a..." Grace's face twisted with the effort of finding the right word. Finally she gave up and just said, "Shit. Complete... shit."

Which made me laugh through the tears, and then I was doing both—laughing and crying and apologising while Grace patted my hand and muttered increasingly creative curse words.

Denise appeared with tea. Claire materialised with tissues. Even Bert shuffled over, looked uncomfortable, and said: "Men are bastards. Most of 'em, anyway. You're better off."

By the time I'd pulled myself together, half the lounge had gathered around me like a concerned family. Which, I supposed, they were.

"Where's Kev?" Maureen asked. "Someone should fetch Kev."

Apparently someone had called Mrs. Patterson, because fifteen minutes later she arrived with Kev in his carrier, looking confused but willing.

"They said emergency?" she asked.

"I'm fine," I tried to say, but my voice broke on the last word.

Mrs. Patterson took one look at my face and opened the carrier. Kev emerged, assessed the situation with one sweeping glance, and walked directly to me.

He climbed onto my lap, and started purring—that deep, rumbling purr that seemed to reach right into your chest and settle something there.

"What happened?" Mrs. Patterson asked gently.

"Bad date," Denise supplied. "Very bad. Walk-out bad."

"Oh, love." Mrs. Patterson sat down beside me.

I sat there, stroking Kev's head, feeling the purr vibrate through my hands. The rage was still there, and the humiliation, and the bone-deep exhaustion of trying and failing and trying again. But Kev's presence made it bearable somehow. Contained.

"I thought he was different," I said finally. "Kev approved of him. Definitely approved. And I thought... I thought maybe this time."

Kev opened one eye, gave me a long look, then closed it again. Still purring. Still there.

"Even Kev gets it wrong sometimes," Maureen said gently. "He's a cat, not a fortune teller."

"He's never got it wrong before."

"Maybe he didn't get it wrong." This was bookish Dorothy, surprisingly. "Maybe this man would have been right for you. But something happened—the phone call—and he made a choice. A bad choice, a cowardly choice. But that's on him, not Kev's judgment."

I thought about that. About how Michael had seemed genuinely interested, genuinely kind, right up until that phone call. Whatever he'd heard had changed something. Made him run.

"I just wish I knew why," I said. "That's the worst part. The not knowing. Was I boring? Did I say something wrong? Was there an actual emergency? I'll never know."

"Does it matter?" Bert asked gruffly. "He buggered off. That tells you everything you need to know about his character. Anyone worth having would have at least said goodbye."

"Bert's right," care assistant Claire said. "Anyone who can just walk away like that isn't someone you want in your life anyway."

They were trying to help, and I appreciated it, but the words felt hollow. Because I had wanted him in my life. For ten beautiful minutes, I'd imagined what that might look like. And then it had evaporated, and I was back to being alone with my ready meals and my quiet flat and my cat-approved dating strategy that apparently didn't work as well as I'd thought.

I stayed late that night, long after the residents had gone to bed. Kev stayed with me, Mrs. Patterson having agreed he could stay over if he wanted to, not that she would or could dictate what he did or didn't do as he came and went as he willed spending more time with us now than he did with her. He moved from my lap to the desk to the windowsill, always within sight, always purring when I needed it.

Around midnight, I wrote in the Good Book:

> Date walk-out incident. Michael walked away mid-conversation and never came back. No explanation. No message. Just... gone.
>
> Staff rallied. Residents rallied. Kev came in on his day off because someone called Mrs. Patterson and told her it was an

emergency. Which it wasn't, not really. But it felt like one.

I'm trying to remember what Denise said last month about absences making room for something better. Trying to believe that Michael walking away means someone else gets to walk in. But right now it just feels like proof that I'm fundamentally un-keepable. That there's something about me that makes people want to leave.

Kev's purring beside me as I write this. He hasn't left, at least. Even when he could have gone to do what cats do at night he stayed. Maybe that's the lesson. The people—or cats—who matter don't leave. Not like that. Not without explanation or apology or decency.

I'm putting dating on hold for a while. Need to remember how to be okay on my own before I can be okay with someone else. And maybe that's fine. Maybe being alone is better than being left.

I closed the book. Kev walked over, sat on it, and stared at me with those amber eyes.

"What?"

He mrowed softly. Not his usual commanding mrow—something gentler. Almost like: *You'll be alright.*

"Will I?"

Another mrow. More certain this time.

I picked him up, buried my face in his fur, and let myself believe him.

Because if a cat who'd been abandoned, who'd lost whatever home he'd once had, who survived on the margins of other people's lives—if that cat could keep showing up, keep caring, keep choosing connection despite the risk—then maybe I could too.

Just not today. Today I'd let myself be sad. Tomorrow I could try again.

Kev purred his agreement, and we sat there in the quiet office, the only sound his rumbling contentment and the distant hum of the building settling into night.

***

I didn't delete the app immediately. I told myself I was just taking a break, regrouping, learning from Kev's (rare) failure of judgment. But really, I'd lost my nerve.

Every profile I looked at seemed to contain a man who would eventually walk away. Who'd say all the right things until the day he didn't. Who'd claim to understand the demands of my work until those demands interfered with his plans.

"You're catastrophising," Denise told me when I admitted this over lunch. "One bad date doesn't mean all men are secretly planning to abandon you mid-coffee."

"Three bad dates. And technically one wasn't even a date—he left before we got that far."

"Fine. Two bad dates. That's honestly not bad for dating apps."

"That's a terrible success rate."

"Depends on your perspective." She stole a chip from my plate. "The point is, you can't let Michael ruin this for you. He's one coward. There are plenty of non-cowards out there."

"Name one."

She thought about it. "Kev."

"Kev is a cat."

"Kev is a better judge of character than either of us. So maybe trust the process?"

I wanted to. I really did. But trust felt like the hardest thing in the world.

***

The week after Michael's disappearing act, I avoided the dating app entirely. Kev, however, had other ideas.

He'd taken to sitting on my phone whenever I tried to use it for anything other than work. Denise found this hilarious.

"The cat's staging an intervention," she said.

"He's being a nuisance."

"He's being your therapist. And he's not charging £60 an hour."

One evening, Kev actually batted my phone off the desk when I opened the app to delete it. Then he sat on the phone, tail wrapped around his paws, staring at me with those amber eyes that somehow conveyed profound disappointment.

"Fine," I told him. "One more try. But if this one's a disaster, I'm done."

I scrolled through profiles while Kev supervised. Most got his usual disinterested yawn. Then one appeared: Adam, history teacher, slightly scruffy, genuine smile.

Kev leaned forward, sniffed the screen, then headbutted my hand decisively.

"Him?"

"Mrow."

"You're sure? Because my track record—"

Another headbutt, more insistent.

I swiped right.

* * *

Kev had become our unofficial counsellor, grief companion, and entertainer-in-residence all at once. He'd already changed so many lives that I'd started to think I'd seen it all. Then came one more reminder that with Kev, you never really had.

April brought warmer weather—proper spring now, not the tentative sort. Bluebells were starting in the shaded corners of the garden, and the cherry tree by the car park had exploded into blossom overnight, as if making up for lost time. April also brought a visit from Janet's daughter, Rachel.

I'd spoken to Rachel a few times on the phone—she lived

a three-hour drive away, had two young children and a demanding job. She'd been wracked with guilt about putting her mother in care, apologetic about not visiting more often, clearly struggling with watching her mother disappear bit by bit.

When Rachel finally made it down on a Saturday afternoon, she was tense and drawn, braced for whatever state she'd find her mother in.

Janet was in the garden with Kev.

It was one of those perfect spring days, warm sun and light breeze, and several residents had opted to sit outside after lunch. Janet was in a wheelchair—she'd had a fall the week before, nothing serious but we were being cautious—with Kev curled up on her lap, both of them dozing in the sunshine.

"Mum?" Rachel approached carefully, and I saw her take in the scene: her mother, peaceful, a cat sleeping on her knees.

Janet opened her eyes. "Rachel! When did you get here?"

The use of her name—the recognition—made Rachel's breath catch. "Just now. I... how are you?"

"I'm lovely." Janet stroked Kev's head. "We're having such a nice time. This is Kev."

"Hi, Kev." Rachel crouched down, blinking back tears. "He's gorgeous, Mum."

"He visits us. Don't you?" This to Kev, who opened one eye, assessed Rachel, and apparently decided she was acceptable. He stretched out a paw and touched her hand.

"Oh," said Rachel, her voice breaking. "Oh, Mum."

They sat like that for an hour, the three of them in the sunshine, talking about small things—the weather, the garden, what Rachel's kids were up to. Janet got confused a few times, called Rachel by her own sister's name once, forgot the thread of conversation and had to be gently redirected. But she was calm. Present. There.

When Rachel stood to leave, I walked her to the car park. She was crying properly now, not bothering to hide it.

"I'm sorry," she said, wiping her face. "I'm not usually this much of a mess."

"You don't need to apologise."

"It's just... that's the best visit I've had with her in a long time. She knew who I was. She was happy. And I know it might not be like that next time, or ever again, but just for today..." She broke down completely.

I let her cry, one hand on her shoulder, while she processed the complicated grief of dementia—mourning someone who's still alive, treasuring moments of clarity because you never know which will be the last.

"The cat," she said finally. "Kev. Does he really come regularly?"

I nodded.

"And he... Mum seems to really respond to him."

"She does. Lots of residents do, but your mum especially. He seems to calm her down when she's agitated. Brings her into the present moment."

Rachel pulled out her phone. "Can I... would it be weird if I took a photo? Of Mum and Kev? I'd like to show my kids, and my brother. I'd like to remember this."

"Of course. Let me do you one better."

I took her back to the garden where Janet was still sitting with Kev, now chatting to Dorothy about something to do with books. I took several photos on Rachel's phone—Janet smiling, Kev looking dignified, the sunshine making everything soft and golden.

But the one that made Rachel cry again was candid: Janet looking down at Kev with such tenderness, her hand mid-stroke, completely unaware of the camera. It could have been taken twenty years ago, before the disease. It was just a woman and a cat and a moment of uncomplicated peace.

"Thank you," Rachel whispered. "Thank you so much."

After she left, I found myself thinking about that photo, about the importance of documenting joy. How we're so good at recording the bad things—the incident reports, the medication errors, the falls and infections and complaints. But what about the moments that make life worth living, even in a place where people come to die?

Good Book:

> Kev sat with Arthur for an hour. Arthur kept saying he could feel his arthritis less when he was stroking the cat. Whether it's true or placebo doesn't matter—he was more mobile this afternoon than I've seen him in weeks.
>
> Janet and Kev were in the garden. Janet clearer today than most days. Rachel's visit went well. The cat is doing something we can't.
>
> Bert claims he still doesn't like cats but I found him giving Kev treats from his pocket. Neither of them acknowledged me. Progress.

That evening, after Rachel had driven away and the residents had settled for the night, I found Tom sitting alone in the conservatory. He was staring at his phone, at the photos we'd taken of his wife and Kev.

"She looks happy," he said without looking up. "In these pictures, she looks like herself."

I sat down beside him. "She was having a good day."

"They're so rare now. The good days." He swiped through the photos slowly. "Used to be the bad days were rare. Then it was fifty-fifty. Now..." He trailed off, not needing to finish.

"I'm sorry."

"Everyone's sorry. Doctors are sorry, nurses are sorry, you're sorry. Everyone's very sorry that my wife is disappearing in front of me while her body keeps going." He wasn't angry—just tired. "But sorry doesn't give me more good days."

"No," I agreed. "It doesn't."

We sat in silence for a moment. Then Tom said, "You know what the worst part is? I keep trying to make memories, to hold onto moments like today, but she won't remember them. This afternoon, with Kev, with our daughter—by tomorrow it'll be gone. And I'll be the only one carrying it. I'm becoming a museum of our life together, and she's just... moving on without me."

His voice broke on the last words.

"That's not quite true," I said gently. "She won't remember the specific moments, but the feelings stay. The sense of being loved, being safe—that doesn't disappear just because the memory does."

"How do you know?"

"Because of how she is with you. Even on her worst days, when she doesn't know your name, she knows you're important. She knows you make her feel safe. That's not memory—that's something deeper."

Tom wiped his eyes. "I hope you're right. God, I hope you're right. Because if all we have left is me remembering for both of us..." He couldn't finish.

"You're not alone in it. We remember too. The staff here, we see her. We see who she is, who she was, who she's trying to be despite everything. And Kev—" I gestured toward the photo on his phone. "Kev remembers. That's why he keeps coming back to her."

"A cat remembers my wife."

"Yes."

Tom laughed, wet and broken but genuine. "That's the strangest comfort I've ever received, and somehow it actually helps."

He stood to leave, then paused. "Thank you. For these photos. For giving us today. Even if Janet won't remember it, even if it's just me carrying it forward—it matters. You gave us something beautiful, and that's rare."

After he left, I stayed in the darkening conservatory, thinking about memory and love and the ways they do and don't intersect. About how we spend so much energy trying to hold onto moments, to preserve them perfectly, when maybe what matters is just having them at all. Being present for them. Letting them change us even if we can't keep them.

I pulled out my phone and looked at the photos I'd taken. Janet and Kev in the sunshine, both of them peaceful, both of them exactly where they needed to be in that moment.

I sent the best one to my own email with the subject line: "Remember this."

Not for Janet, who couldn't. Not even for Tom, who would never forget. For me. For the days when the work felt too hard and the losses too frequent and the question "does any of this matter?" grew too loud to ignore.

This moment mattered. Kev mattered. Love mattered, even when—especially when—it's temporary, fragile, doomed from the start. Maybe that's the only kind of love there is.

Watching Rachel drive away that day, I realised how often Kev's gift wasn't in what he did but in what he allowed.

People found their way back to each other around him. Even if it was only for an hour, a day, a breath — it was enough. And slowly, impossibly, I began to believe it might be enough for me, too.

***

We discovered Kev's nocturnal side in mid April, though "discovered" suggests we found it deliberately rather than stumbling into it at two in the morning.

Mabel had survived more than most people could imagine. Born in 1934, she'd been seven years old when the Blitz began, living in Bethnal Green with her mother and younger brother while her father served somewhere over in

North Africa. She could still describe, in terrifying detail, the sound of bombers overhead—that particular droning hum that meant you had minutes, maybe seconds, to get underground.

I never did quite understand why she hadn't been evacuated like most East End kids.

"Like giant wasps," she'd say. "Angry wasps coming to sting the whole city."

At Rivermead, she was gentle and polite by day. A tiny woman who still did her hair in pin curls every night, who said "please" and "thank you" for everything, who apologised if she thought she was being any trouble at all.

But as dusk fell, something shifted.

Ruth, our night shift supervisor, first mentioned it to me on a Monday morning. "Mabel's up half the night. Walking the corridors, checking doors, getting agitated. Keeps asking where the shelter is."

"Sundowning?" I suggested, though Mabel didn't have dementia.

"I don't think so. It's more specific than that. She's not confused about where she is—she knows this is Rivermead. But she's convinced she needs to check the shelter. Says there are young children inside and someone has to make sure they're safe."

I went to speak with Mabel that afternoon. Found her in the conservatory, bright-eyed and cheerful, working on a crossword.

"How are you sleeping, Mabel?"

"Oh, fine, dear. Though I do get up sometimes. Old habits." She smiled that apologetic smile. "I'm not making a nuisance of myself, am I?"

"Not at all. Ruth mentioned you've been checking the doors at night?"

Something flickered across her face—half-memory, half-fear. "Just making sure. You have to check, you see. During the war, we had air raid wardens who'd walk the streets making sure everyone was in the shelters. My father did it before he was called up. I used to go with him sometimes."

"That must have been frightening."

"It was. But someone had to do it. You couldn't just leave people above ground. The bombs—" She stopped, looked down at her hands. "They made such dreadful sounds when they fell. Whistling. You'd hear the whistle and count. One, two, three. If you got to four, you knew it hadn't hit you."

"Mabel—"

"I'm fine during the day," she said quickly. "It's just at night, when it gets dark and quiet. I hear things. I know it's not real, not anymore, but I hear them. And I think: someone should check. Someone should make sure everyone's safe."

We tried everything for her. Warm milk before bed. Lavender spray on her pillows. Night lights. A radio playing gentle music. Night manager Ruth would sit with her, talking her through the anxiety, reminding her the war was over, she was safe, everyone was safe.

Nothing helped. Around two a.m., like clockwork, Mabel would slip from bed and begin her patrol. Barefoot, in her nightdress and dressing gown, she'd walk the corridors whispering the same thing: "I have to check the shelter. The babies are inside. Someone has to check."

It broke my heart.

Then one wet Wednesday night in early June (the rain was rehearsing for Wimbledon fortnight), Ruth rang me at home. I answered on the second ring, instantly awake, heart racing with that particular adrenaline that comes with three a.m. phone calls.

"Dawn, don't panic. Everyone's safe. But you need to hear this."

"What happened?"

"Mabel managed to open the garden door—you know

that old fire exit we barely use? She must have figured out the push bar. By the time I found her, she was standing in the middle of the lawn in her nightdress. Barefoot. It's been raining. She was soaked through."

"Jeez. Is she—"

"She's fine. Not even cold, somehow. But Dawn—Kev was with her."

I sat up properly. "What?"

"The cat. He was sitting right beside her. Just... there. Like he'd followed her out."

"How did he even get out there?"

"You know that cat flap we installed in the fire door? For emergencies? I think he heard her and came through. He was circling her legs when I found them, tail brushing against her calves, and she was just standing there pointing at the sky, talking to him."

"Talking about what?"

Ruth's voice softened. "The stars. She was telling the cat about the stars. How they were the same ones she used to look at during the blackout. How her mother would tell her to look up when the sirens got too loud, find the brightest star and make a wish."

I drove to Rivermead in my onesie. Found Mabel in her room, dry now, wrapped in a blanket, sipping tea that Ruth had made. Kev was curled up on her bed, refusing to leave.

"I'm so sorry," Mabel said when she saw me. "I didn't mean to cause trouble."

"You didn't cause any trouble. I just wanted to make sure you were alright."

"The cat took me to see the stars," she said simply. "He said it was safe."

I glanced at Ruth, who shrugged slightly.

"Did he?"

"Mm. He was sitting by my door—you know how he does sometimes, just waiting. And I was having one of my nights, hearing things, getting worried. So I followed him. He went straight to that door, you see. Knew exactly where he was going."

"Mabel, you can't go outside in the middle of the night. It's not safe."

"But it was safe. Because of the cat. He showed me the stars—they're all the same ones, you know. From London, from the war. Same constellations. I'd forgotten that. Forgotten that no matter how bad things get, the stars stay the same."

She sipped her tea, looking more peaceful than I'd seen her in weeks. "My mother used to say that. When we couldn't sleep from the noise, from the fear. She'd take us outside after the all-clear and show us the stars. 'See?' she'd say. 'Still there. Still shining. Can't bomb the stars.'"

Kev opened one eye, looked at me, closed it again. Extraordinarily pleased with himself.

After Mabel had settled back to sleep, I found Ruth in the office.

"This can't happen again," I said. "What if she'd fallen? What if we hadn't found her?"

"I know. But Dawn—you should have seen her out there. She wasn't confused or agitated. She was calm. The calmest I've seen her at night since she arrived."

I looked at Kev, who'd followed us to the office and was now washing his face with studied indifference.

"We need to make it safe," I said finally. "If this is going to be a thing, we need to make it safe."

So we did. We created a 'night garden protocol'—my phrasing, which Denise immediately mocked but couldn't improve upon. At half past nine, before the late medication round, we'd check if Mabel was having one of her anxious evenings. If she was, we'd offer her the option: would she like to do her patrol?

"We can go together," Ruth would say. "You, me, and if

he's here, the cat."

The first time we tried it officially, Mabel looked uncertain. "You'll think I'm mad."

"I think you're someone who needs to make sure everyone's safe," Ruth said gently. "And that's not mad. That's kind."

So they went—Mabel in her dressing gown and proper slippers this time, Ruth beside her, and Kev appearing as if summoned. They'd walk the path through the garden, Mabel checking doors and windows from outside, making sure everything was secure.

And she'd talk. Talk about the air raid shelter at the end of her street, how it always smelled of damp earth and fear. About Mrs. Henderson from number twelve who'd bring her knitting and try to keep spirits up. About the night they heard the bomb that hit the school three streets over, how the ground had shaken and the lights had flickered and gone out.

"We sang," she told Kev, who padded along beside her like a small orange guardian. "When the lights went out and we couldn't see anything, Mrs. Henderson started singing 'Pack Up Your Troubles' and we all joined in. Even those of us who'd been crying. Because if you're singing, you're not dead yet, are you?"

Kev would mrow occasionally, as if agreeing or encouraging. And gradually, over the course of ten minutes, Mabel's anxiety would ease. The tight set of her shoulders would relax. Her breathing would slow.

By the time they came back inside, she was ready for bed.

"Thank you for helping me patrol," she'd tell Kev seriously. "Can't do it properly without a partner."

He'd mrow once more, then follow her to her room, where he'd stay until she fell asleep.

The staff came to cherish those ten minutes or so. It became the calmest part of the night shift—the sound of

Mabel's voice carrying softly through the garden, Kev's bell tinkling as he walked, the night birds settling, the world briefly at peace.

One night I stayed late specifically to observe. Watched from the office window as they made their circuit—woman, nurse, cat under the vast cosmos. Mabel's voice was too quiet to hear from inside, but I could see her gesturing at the sky, pointing out constellations to Kev. Or perhaps, I wondered, he was pointing out constellations to her.

Ruth told me later what she'd said: "That's the Plough. And there—that bright one—that's the North Star. My mother said it's the most important one because it never moves. Everything else spins around it, but it stays constant. That's what you look for when you're lost."

When they came back in, Mabel was smiling. Actually smiling.

"Good patrol?" I asked.

"Very good. No bombs tonight. Everyone's safe." She patted Kev's head. "The cat keeps watch, you see. So I don't have to worry so much."

After she went to bed, I sat with Ruth and Kev in the quiet office.

"This is insane," I said. "We're enabling a nightly patrol routine based on eighty-year-old war trauma, facilitated by a cat."

"Is it working?"

I thought about it. About how Mabel slept six, sometimes seven solid hours after her patrols—unheard of before. About how her daytime anxiety had decreased. About how she'd started eating better, engaging more, living more fully because she was actually sleeping.

"Yes," I admitted. "It's working."

"Then who cares if it's insane?"

Kev mrowed his agreement.

Mrs. Patterson, when I explained the situation the next

day, just laughed.

"Course he does night shifts. Just make sure Ruth gives him some treats. Night work deserves overtime pay."

So we did. Kev got extra treats on nights when Mabel needed her patrol, which he accepted with regal condescension, as if we'd finally recognised his true value.

And Mabel? Mabel slept. Finally, after months of broken nights and war-ghosts and anxiety that no amount of reassurance could touch, she slept.

Because a cat understood what we'd missed: she didn't need to forget the war. She needed to finish her patrol. To know that the young children—those long-ago children in the long-ago shelter—were safe. That someone was keeping watch. That the bombs had stopped falling and the stars were still there, constant and unchanging in the dark.

Kev gave her that. And in return, she gave him a purpose he seemed to take as seriously as any he'd held before.

Every war needs its watchers. And if ours wore orange fur and a purple collar, well. He did the job, and he did it well.

That was all that mattered.

If Kev was the guardian of Rivermead by day, at night he became its watchman, keeping the ghosts quiet until morning.

Mabel slept seven hours straight after her 'patrol' with Kev. Perhaps we all sleep easier knowing someone is quietly keeping watch. That someone—even a scruffy ginger cat—cares enough to make sure we're safe. Maybe that's what Mabel needed all along: not to stop checking, but to share the burden. To know she's not alone in it anymore.

***

That summer draped Rivermead in a lazy warmth, the scent of freshly cut grass drifting through open windows as Kev made his rounds.

The residents had nicknames for him—Maureen called him "Doctor Whiskers," while Bert insisted he was "the boss." I watched Kev from my office, paperwork piling up, and wondered how a stray had become our heartbeat.

Kev's presence had become part of our daily rhythm, as natural as tea at three.

The residents planned their days around his visits. I watched them sometimes—Dorothy saving her best chair for him, Bert sneaking him scraps from his lunch—and wondered if the cat knew how much he'd changed us—how he'd turned a place of endings into a place of beginnings, one purr at a time.

Afternoons became sacred time—activities were scheduled around Kev, not the other way around.

"Can't do physio at two," Arthur would say. "That's when Kev comes."

"My daughter wants to visit Thursday," Eleanor told me. "Can she come before two? Before Kev?"

Even the kitchen staff adjusted. They started saving scraps—tiny pieces of cooked chicken, drops of cream—which residents would secret away in pockets to offer to Kev. We had to have a staff meeting about it.

"He's on a special diet," I explained, trying not to laugh at the guilty faces around the table. "Mrs. Patterson is very careful about what he eats. Too many treats will upset his stomach."

"But he likes the chicken," Margaret protested.

"I know he does. But we have to think about what's best for him, not just what he wants."

It was like reasoning with parents about spoiling a grandchild. Eventually, we reached a compromise: approved treats only, kept in the kitchen, doled out sparingly. Kev would survive.

The impact of his visits was starting to show up in unexpected ways. Our medication usage for anti-anxiety drugs had dropped. Incidents of aggressive behaviour in residents with dementia had decreased. Even our staff retention had improved—people wanted to work somewhere with a cat.

"It's the Kev effect," Denise joked, but she wasn't entirely wrong.

I started getting calls from other care homes, managers who'd heard about our therapy cat programme. Could I share our documentation? Our protocols? How had we made it work?

I shared everything freely. The risk assessments, the family consent forms, the training materials. I told them about Kev's arrival, how we'd started small, how we'd let him set the pace.

"But here's the thing," I always added. "You can't force it. The animal has to choose you. Kev chose us. We just had the good sense to say yes."

Some of them got it. Others didn't, came back months later complaining that they'd tried to bring in a cat and it hadn't worked, the cat was stressed, the residents weren't interested.

"Wrong cat," I'd say. "Or wrong timing. You can't manufacture this."

**

The garden bloomed in earnest now—roses climbing the trellis, lavender beginning to purple, the grass thick enough that it needed cutting once a week. Windows stayed open, letting in the sound of birdsong and the smell of cut grass.

Adam and I had arranged to meet for coffee on a Thursday straight after work. For some reason, I was more nervous about this first date than I'd been about any of the others. I'd already changed my mind three times about what I was going to wear for our first meeting—highly unusual for me—and had brought in a number of outfits from home to change into.

"He looks nice," Claire said when I showed her Adam's photo: the history teacher who had passed Kev's online vetting process and who I'd been chatting to since.

"Too normal looking!" interrupted Denise. "That's automatically suspicious."

"But Kev was keen." I mused.

"Perfect for you then - but seriously now, Dawn, is the cat dating him or are you?"

'He seems nice on the phone." I said lamely as I went to change into my fourth outfit of the day.

"They all do at first!" Denise rolled her eyes ominously. 'But don't let me put you off."

I was struggling with the zip of my red dress when Kev appeared in the doorway to my bedroom at the care home, tail swishing.

"You don't get to judge," I told him. "You lick your own fur."

He jumped onto the bed and promptly sat on the matching jacket I'd just ironed.

"That one's out then."

He then proceeded to veto my two second choices by sitting on them with the dedication of a personal stylist who despised my taste.

By the time I left work, I was late, flustered, and covered in cat hair.

Adam was at the coffee shop, ready waiting. He smiled when he saw me—not the polite smile of someone keeping score of tardiness, but genuine warmth.

His dating photo hadn't done him justice. He was even more gorgeous in real life. I tried my best to play it cool but my heart was racing ten to a dozen.

"Rough shift?" His warm eyes met mine and my heart did another little flip.

"Is it that obvious?"

"You've got that look. The one that says you've been managing seventeen crises simultaneously while pretending everything's fine."

I laughed despite myself. "That's disturbingly accurate."

We found a corner table, away from the noise. For the first twenty minutes, I couldn't quite settle—half-expecting the home to call with some new disaster. Adam waited patiently, sipping his latte, not pushing.

Finally he said, "Tell me about the worst part of today."

Not the best part. Not small talk about weather or weekend plans. The worst part.

So I told him. About Mrs. O'Neal's daughter shouting at me because her mother's cardigan had gone missing (it was in the laundry). About the medication error—not serious, caught immediately, but still requiring incident reports and family notification. About feeling like I was constantly one step behind, never quite good enough.

"And the thing is," I said, "I love this job. I really do. But some days it feels like I'm bailing out the Titanic with a teaspoon."

Adam was quiet for a moment. Then: "My nan was in a home. Before she died. It was years ago. But I remember visiting. Seeing the staff—people like you—doing impossible jobs for not enough money and even less recognition. My nan's favourite carer was this woman called Brenda who always remembered that Nan liked her tea lukewarm, not hot. Sounds tiny, but it meant so much. Made Nan feel seen."

He looked at me directly. "You do that. I can tell. You see people."

Something in my chest loosened. "Kev helps."

Adam frowned a moment at my mentioning another man's name and I realised he didn't know who Kev was yet.

I grinned, brushing off a long orange hair from my sleeve I'd missed with the roller. "Kev. My colleague. He's very clingy."

Adam stared at the pet hair and grinned. "Dog or cat?

"Cat."

"Then he's forgiven."

I promptly told Adam all about Kev,

He laughed. "So he's your supervisor?"

"More like a furry line manager," I said. "He's better at it than I am, honestly. He just knows who needs him."

"I'd love to meet him one day. If that's allowed."

"You want to meet our cat."

"Your colleague," Adam corrected. "I want to meet your ginger colleague who apparently runs the place."

We talked until closing time. About his teaching—he had the same exhausted love for it that I had for care work. About his students, some of whom came from difficult homes and needed someone to believe in them. About his ex, briefly (amicable split, two years ago, no drama). About my ex, even more briefly (less amicable, more drama, best forgotten).

When he walked me to my car, the evening felt balmy and full of promise.

"I'd like to do this again," he said. "If you would."

"Even knowing I'll probably cancel half the time because of work?"

"Even knowing that." He paused. "Look, I'm not going to pretend I understand what you do. But I'd like to try. If you'll let me."

I kissed him. Not planned, not smooth—just a sudden overwhelming need to be closer to someone who saw the work and didn't run.

He kissed back, gentle and unhurried, one hand cupping my face like I was something precious.

When we pulled apart, I was smiling properly for the first time in days.

Driving home, I felt something I hadn't felt in years:

hope. Not the naive kind, but the hard-won kind that comes from being disappointed and trying anyway.

My phone buzzed just as I walked through my front door. A text from Adam as if he were psychic: *Made it home safe? x*

I replied: *Yes. Thanks for tonight. x*

Three dots appeared, then: *Thanks for trusting me with the hard parts. x*

I saved that message.

Back at work the next day, it seemed as if Kev was waiting for me to come in to pounce on me. He gave me the slow blink of feline interrogation. *Well?*

"It was nice," I said. "No disasters. Adam didn't mention fluoride or cryptocurrency once."

Kev wound between my legs, purring loudly enough to rattle my keys. Endorsement received.

"We have another date booked in…" I paused. "And he wants to meet you."

I could have sworn then that Kev winked at me.

After Kev's interrogation, it was time for the rest of the staff:

"Was he tall?" Claire demanded.

"Did he pay?" asked Denise.

"Does Kev approve?" called Bert from his doorway.

"He does," I said, trying to look dignified.

Bert grunted. "Then he's alright."

Good Book—

Kev's intuition extends beyond residents. Possibly clairvoyant. Requesting funding for matchmaking cat pilot scheme.

***

Grace had arrived in February, and she'd arrived angry.

Seventy-three years old, the former headmistress was a stroke survivor. The stroke had left her with limited mobility on her right side and, more devastatingly for someone who'd spent her life wielding words like weapons, significant aphasia. She knew what she wanted to say but couldn't get the words out, or they'd come out wrong, jumbled, her brain and mouth no longer in agreement.

The frustration was eating her alive.

"I don't... the thing... FUCK!" This was Grace's primary mode of communication in those first weeks. She'd try to ask for something, fail, and the rage would erupt. She threw things. Refused medication. Shouted at staff in garbled sentences that made her even angrier when we couldn't understand.

Her daughter, Kathryn, was at her wits' end. "She was so articulate before. She gave speeches. She ran a school of four hundred pupils. And now she can't even ask for a cup of tea without..."

"It's early days," I said, though I didn't feel as optimistic as I sounded. "Speech therapy will help."

But therapy was slow, and Grace's anger was fast and hot and consuming.

The other residents started avoiding her. Staff drew the short straw to work with her. Even I, who prided myself on patience, found myself dreading interactions with Grace, bracing for the inevitable explosion.

Then one Monday afternoon, Kev met Grace.

He'd been doing his usual rounds—Maureen, Dorothy, Eleanor, another new resident named Margaret who'd taken to carrying cat treats in her pocket—when he suddenly stopped, ears swivelling toward the conservatory where Grace sat alone, glowering at a word search puzzle she couldn't do anymore, tears of frustration tracking down her face.

Kev padded over and jumped onto the table next to her puzzle book.

"Ge... get... cat. GO." Grace tried to swat him away.

Kev sat down and stared at her.

"I said... you... GO."

Kev began washing his face.

Grace's hand hovered, uncertain. Then she tried again: "Don't... I don't... want..." The words tangled up, and I saw the rage building behind her eyes.

Kev stopped washing and looked at her. Just looked, with those amber eyes that seemed to see everything.

And something in Grace cracked.

"I can't," she said, the words coming out clear for once. "I can't do this."

Kev stood up, stepped carefully over the puzzle book, and butted his head against her hand.

Grace started to cry—not the angry tears of before, but something deeper, more raw.

Her left hand came up and touched Kev's head, tentative at first, then more firmly. It was a quiet moment, but it felt monumental, like watching someone find their way back to themselves after being lost for so long.

"I used to... words... had so many..." She was crying harder now, her face crumpling. "All gone. All... fuck. Gone."

Kev climbed into her lap—he was getting quite good at reading situations—and pushed his head under her chin.

Denise, who'd been watching from the doorway, muttered, 'If he starts charging for therapy sessions, we're all in trouble."

We watched as Grace cried into Kev's fur, her good hand clutching him like a lifeline, words breaking over her in waves—some clear, most not, all of them saturated with loss and fear and grief.

Kev stayed perfectly still, purring steadily, a warm weight that demanded nothing and offered everything.

When Grace finally stopped crying, she looked exhausted but somehow lighter. She kept one hand on Kev's back, moving in slow strokes.

"Nice," she said clearly. "You're... nice."

Kev mrowed his agreement.

"What's... name?"

"That's Kev," I said, moving closer now.

Grace frowned, processing this. Then: "Kev. Stupid name."

I couldn't help it—I laughed. And after a moment, so did Grace. It was rusty, like she'd forgotten how, but it was definitely a laugh.

"You're absolutely right," I said. "It is a stupid name."

"But... good cat."

"The best cat."

Grace looked down at Kev, then back at me. When she spoke again, the words came slowly but clearly: "Can he... come... Tomorrow?"

"He'll be here. Two o'clock, regularly as clockwork."

"Good." She went back to stroking Kev, and I noticed something: her right hand, the affected one, was moving. Not much, just small twitches, but movement nonetheless. Following the motion of her left hand, remembering.

Over the following weeks, something remarkable happened. Grace still got frustrated, still struggled with words, still had days where the anger consumed her. But when Kev arrived, she had a focus. Something to work toward.

"Kev," she'd practice, working with the speech therapist. "The cat. Kev the cat." Simple phrases, over and over, so she'd be ready when he arrived.

And it worked. Slowly, agonisingly slowly, Grace's language began to return. Not perfectly—it never would be perfect—but she could make herself understood. Could ask for what she needed. Could tell Kathryn about her day, even if it took twice as long as it used to.

"It's the motivation," the speech therapist told me. "She wants to be able to talk to the cat. It sounds ridiculous, but it's working. She's trying harder than any patient I've had in a long time."

One day in July, I found Grace sitting with Kev, reading to him from a large-print book. The words came haltingly, with long pauses when she got stuck, but she was reading. Actually reading.

"'The cat sat on the mat,'" she read. Then looked at Kev. "Stupid book. You're... more... clever than this."

Kev mrowed.

"I know. Insul... insulting." She stumbled over the word but got there. "Tomorrow I'll bring... better book. Dick... Dickens maybe."

"Dickens?" I couldn't hide my surprise.

Grace looked at me with something of her old authority. "I taught... English. Forty years. Not going to read... baby books... to a cat with taste."

"Of course not," I said, grinning.

A couple of days later, Grace had a copy of Great Expectations, and she spent an hour reading chapter one to Kev, who listened with apparent fascination. She had to stop frequently, had to sound out words she'd once known perfectly, but she persisted.

And Kev stayed, patient and present, the most attentive audience she could have asked for.

"Thank you," Kathryn said to me one day, after finding her mother reading aloud, Kev curled up beside her.

The lounge was warm—too warm—with afternoon sun pouring through south-facing windows. Someone had brought in lilacs from the garden, their heavy perfume almost cloying. A bee buzzed against the glass, trying to escape, its drone the only sound besides Grace's reading to Kev.

"I know it's silly to thank someone for a cat, but he's given her something back. Some part of herself."

"It's not silly at all," I said.

But privately, I was thinking: Kev wasn't giving anything back. He was helping Grace find what had been there all along, buried under trauma and frustration. He was just showing her the way.

I wrote in the Good Book:
Kev has a way of making the impossible feel simple, of reminding us that healing doesn't always come in grand gestures. Sometimes, it's just a purr and a warm paw.

That evening, Denise rallied the staff for a group activity—painting plant pots for the garden, Kev watching from the window ledge like a ginger foreman.

"He's got us all well trained," Claire laughed, brushing paint off her scrubs. The laughter felt lighter than it had in months, a sign the home was steadier since Kev's arrival. Staff turnover had slowed; even Denise, who'd eyed jobs elsewhere, stayed put.

I was distracted, though. Adam had texted about our second date—a picnic, weather permitting. As I watched the staff tease each other, paint smudged on their noses, I smiled. But the laughter softened, and Kev's steady gaze caught mine, reminding me to trust my heart again.

***

Seeing Adam again felt different. Easy. No scripts, no second-guessing. We met for a picnic, and the weather gods decided to be kind to us for once, proving that not only Kev but the Universe may be willing for us to work out.

This time I was not covered in cat hair - at least I didn't think so - but I knew instinctively Adam wouldn't mind one bit if I were. I'd already asked my fluffy personal stylist what to wear before the date so no need for veto dramas and it turned out the cat didn't have bad taste.

Adam and I talked about books, work, and the absurdity of online dating. I stopped waiting for disaster; he stopped trying to impress. He didn't need to, There was something about him that just felt so right.

For the first time in years, I wasn't performing. I wasn't someone's boss, daughter, or potential disappointment—I was just me.

I didn't call it love, not yet though my heart was definitely stirring. It was something quieter—belonging, maybe. And after everything that had happened, quiet felt like the right kind of miracle.

***

Music therapy had never really taken off at Rivermead. The sessions were well-intentioned but stiff—half the residents couldn't hear properly, and the rest refused to sing anything written after 1969.

The new music therapist arrived one Friday with a keyboard, a box of shakers, and the sort of grin that made the residents suspicious.

"I'm Sam," he announced. "And today we're going to make some noise!"

Arthur muttered, "God help us," under his breath.

Sam launched into *You Are My Sunshine*. Half the room stared. Dorothy pretended to adjust her hearing aid. Grace crossed her arms.

And then the side door opened and in padded Kev, curious as ever. He jumped onto the empty keyboard stool, placed one paw squarely on a key, and produced a single, dramatic *boing*.

"Ah," said Sam gamely. "Our accompanist has arrived."

Laughter rippled through the room. Grace, who'd been scowling in her wheelchair, actually smiled.

Kev pressed another key—two notes this time, both perfectly in tune. Sam harmonised with it, eyes wide in mock awe.

"Everyone, follow the cat!"

Sam began to play, and Kev—purely by chance or cosmic

timing—stepped onto the keyboard at just the right moments, adding random discordant notes that somehow worked. The residents dissolved into giggles.

It was ridiculous, and it worked. Maureen started clapping, Bert tapped the table with his pen, Grace actually hummed. Joyce nodded along. By the chorus, the room was roaring, and Kev, now sprawled across the keyboard, contributed random chords that somehow made the whole thing joyful rather than chaotic.

"Go on, sing!" Sam urged rattling a shaker. And they did. Off-key, too loud, gloriously alive.

When we finished, the residents were breathless and beaming. Grace leaned towards me and said, halting but clear, "Best… music… ever."

Afterwards, Sam wiped his eyes. "I've never had an audience like this. Or a colleague with whiskers."

From that week on, Sam called it *The Kev Choir*. They sang everything from wartime ballads to The Beatles. Kev was always there—sometimes supervising from a windowsill, sometimes adding a pawful of discordant brilliance, sometimes curled on someone's lap, purring a low bass line.

If joy has a sound, it's a roomful of off-key pensioners and one ginger cat hitting middle C.

Good Book:
Sam's first music session became a full-blown concert. Grace sang. Bert hummed. Kev accompanied. Joy can be loud, even in a care home.

* * *

The garden hummed with bees, their buzz drifting through open windows as summer settled over Rivermead.

My 'dating life'—such as it was—had become staff—and resident—entertainment.

The residents had appointed themselves as my collective

romantic advisors, offering wisdom that ranged from touching to terrifying. Maureen told me to look for kind eyes. Dorothy said intelligence mattered more than looks. Florence—prickly Florence—told me to make sure he could argue properly.

"Anyone who agrees with everything you say is either lying or spineless. You want someone with opinions."

But it was Bert's advice that stuck with me.

"Just bring your new fella here," he said one Wednesday while Kev dozed on his lap. "Let us meet him. We'll know in five minutes if he's worth keeping."

"I'm not bringing a date to a care home, Bert."

"Why not? We're your family, aren't we? Family meets the boyfriend. That's how it works."

"He's not my boyfriend. I've only met him three times—"

I wasn't going to tell Bert those three times had all been utterly brilliant.

"All the more reason. Bring him here. We'll tell you what we think. And if the cat doesn't like him, you'll know straight away to stop wasting any more of your time on him. Better that then find out he's no good and getting your heart broken."

The idea was absurd. Except it wasn't, not really. These people knew me better than my actual family did. They'd seen me at my worst—exhausted, frustrated, crying over residents who'd died — and Michael who left me high and dry in a coffee shop. They'd also seen me at my best. If anyone could judge whether someone was right for me, it was them.

And Kev. Obviously Kev.

If Kev liked Adam, maybe he was worth holding onto. From the moment I first saw Adam in person, it felt like I'd come home. There was something about his smile—I can't quite explain it. It was like an inner recognition, as if my heart had always known him somehow.

But Kev had this uncanny ability to see things in people that others missed—his instincts were sharper than any fortune teller. He had a knack for sniffing out the best—and sometimes the worst—in people. There weren't many folks Kev avoided. He had this way of seeing the potential in even the grumpiest souls, as if to say, *"Hey, I see the good in you; you're worth changing."* He was a furry 'Be Kind' meme in action. Except for with one person. Every time Phil, the parcel courier, showed up, Kev would hiss and bare his teeth. Later, Phil was convicted of some truly awful crimes—things I don't even like to think about. Kev was spot on.

Adam and I hadn't said the 'L' word yet—it felt way too soon—but I sensed, hoped, that whatever this was, it was mutual. I was walking on cloud nine, even though I was pulling double shifts and utterly exhausted. Still, I didn't want any nasty surprises to bring me crashing back to reality. You know what they say: forewarned is forearmed. So, I decided to take Bert's advice. And Denise's. And Claire's. I'd consult Mystic Kev.

When Adam suggested meeting for a Costa after work on a Thursday, something made me say: "Actually, would you mind coming to Rivermead? I need to drop off some paperwork anyway. We could have coffee in the staff room."

There was a pause. Then: "Is this a test? Because it feels like a test."

"It's not a test. I just... I spend most of my life there. If you're going to understand me, you need to understand the place."

"Fair enough. What time?"

"Four-thirty? That's when Kev should still be here."

"The matchmaker cat? Definitely coming now. Need to meet my competition."

When I told the staff, Denise's grin was positively feral.

"Oh, this is happening. We're all staying late. This is better than television."

"You're not all staying late. It's not a spectator sport."

"Course not. We'll be very discreet. Invisible, even. You won't even know we're there."

"Denise—"

"Too late. Already texted everyone. Claire's bringing biscuits."

I tried to manage expectations with the residents too, but that was equally futile.

"We'll be on our best behaviour," Maureen promised, which somehow sounded more threatening than reassuring.

By the time Thursday arrived, I was genuinely nervous. Not about Adam—about subjecting him to what was essentially a group interview with twenty elderly people and a judgmental cat.

I met him in the car park at 4.30 PM, Adam punctual as always. He'd brought flowers.

"For you," he said, handing them over. "Or should I give them to Kev? I'm unclear on the power dynamics here."

I laughed despite my nerves. "Split the difference. These are for the staff room. You can give Kev your approval in person."

As we walked toward the entrance, I tried to prepare him. "Just so you know, the residents are very invested in my personal life. And by invested, I mean intrusive. And the cat—"

"Takes his responsibilities seriously. You've mentioned. I'm ready."

He was not ready.

The first sign should have been the unusual number of residents in the lounge at four-thirty on a Thursday. Normally half of them would be napping or in their rooms. Today, the room was packed. Every chair occupied. Every pair of eyes trained on the entrance.

"Subtle," I muttered.

Adam squeezed my hand briefly. "It's fine. I've faced

tougher crowds. Year 11s on a Friday afternoon are essentially feral."

We walked in. Twenty pairs of eyes swivelled to follow us. The silence was deafening.

"Everyone, this is Adam. Adam teaches history. He's just here to—"

I didn't get to finish because Kev chose that moment to make his entrance through the French windows. He paused in the doorway, tail high, and surveyed the scene with what could only be described as satisfaction. He'd known. Somehow, the little bastard had known this was happening.

He walked directly to Adam, sat down at his feet, and stared up at him.

The room held its collective breath.

Adam, to his credit, didn't panic. He crouched down, making himself smaller, less threatening. "So this is the famous Kev," Adam said, crouching. "I've heard you run the place."

Kev continued staring. Assessing. The silence stretched on.

Then, after what felt like several years but was probably ten seconds, Kev stood up, walked forward, and butted his head against Adam's hand.

The room exhaled.

"Well," said Bert from his chair. "That's settled then."

Adam looked up at me, confused. "What's settled?"

"You passed," Maureen explained, beaming. "Kev likes you. That means we like you."

"I don't get a say in this?" I asked.

"Course you do, love," Dorothy said. "But you already liked him or you wouldn't have brought him here. We're just confirming."

Kev, apparently deciding Adam had been adequately vetted, jumped into his lap without warning. Adam caught him instinctively, adjusted his weight, and started stroking his head with the unconscious competence of someone who actually liked cats.

"He's heavier than he looks," Adam said.

"Muscular," I replied. "All that therapeutic work."

"Clearly. Hello, mate. Heard you've been quality-controlling Dawn's dating life. Appreciate the thorough process."

Kev began to purr—not his polite social purr, but the deep, rumbling purr he reserved for people he genuinely approved of.

"That's a yes," Bert announced. "Definite yes. Cat's made his decision."

"Does the cat always make decisions this quickly?" Adam asked, still stroking Kev's head.

"Only when he's sure," Grace said, her words coming more easily than usual. "He... knows. Always knows."

"No pressure!" smirked Denise.

What followed was possibly the strangest hour of my life. Adam ended up sitting in the lounge with Kev on his lap, being interviewed by residents who had absolutely no sense of appropriate boundaries.

"What are your intentions?" Florence asked directly.

"Toward Dawn? Honourable. Toward the cat? To stay on his good side."

Adam, somehow, handled it all with grace. He answered the intrusive questions with humour. He asked about their lives. He listened when Dorothy started telling a story about her late husband. He didn't check his phone once.

And Kev stayed on his lap the entire time, purring steadily, occasionally stretching up to headbutt Adam's chin as if reminding everyone: *I chose this one. Pay attention.*

After about an hour, Bert said: "Right, you've passed. You can take her for coffee now."

"I can?"

"Yes. You're not completely useless. Cat likes you, which

means you've got potential. Don't waste it."

"I'll do my best."

As we walked to the staff room—finally—for actual coffee, Adam was shaking his head in amazement.

"That was the most thorough vetting I've ever received."

"I'm so sorry. I didn't think they'd all—"

"Are you kidding? That was brilliant. When was the last time anyone cared enough about you to interrogate your dates?"

I thought about it. "Never, actually."

"Exactly. You've got twenty people in there who love you enough to make sure I'm not a dickhead. That's pretty special."

We sat in the staff room—empty, thankfully, Denise having herded everyone away despite her earlier threats. Kev followed us, jumped onto the table between us, and settled down like a chaperone.

"So," Adam said. "I passed?"

"Apparently."

"How do you feel about that?"

I looked at him properly. At his kind eyes and his slightly nervous smile and the way he'd handled the ambush with humour instead of running. At how Kev was still there, still purring, still certain.

"I think," I said carefully, "that Kev might be onto something."

"Just Kev?"

"The residents too. They're good judges of character."

"And you? What do you think?"

I reached across the table, scratched Kev behind his ears, felt the purr intensify. "I think I'd like to do this again. Properly. Without the interview panel."

"Coffee? Or the thorough background check?"

"Coffee. Or dinner sounds good. Though fair warning—you'll probably get randomly interrogated every time you visit now. They've decided you're 'approved.' That comes with ongoing monitoring."

"I can live with that." He grinned. "Besides, I need to maintain my standing with Kev. Can't have him revoking his endorsement."

As if understanding, Kev stood up, walked across the table, and pushed his head against Adam's hand once more. Message clear: *Keep this one. He'll do.*

"Alright, mate. Thanks for the reference. I'll give you the catnip later!" Adam joked.

"He won't forgive you if you don't bring any, mind!" I smiled.

The next day, after the residents had finished debriefing me ("He's lovely, dear." "Nice eyes." "Seems reliable." "I approve."), I found Bert in his room.

"Thank you," I said. "For suggesting I bring him here."

"Course. Had to make sure he was worth your time. Is he?"

"I think so."

"Good. Cat thinks so too, and he's never wrong." Bert paused. "Man should be vetted properly. Had to get my Margaret's father's approval before I could court her. Took three months and a bottle of decent whisky. Worth it, though."

Bert nodded, smiling at sweet memories. "You deserve someone who doesn't run away, Dawn. Someone who sees all this—" he gestured vaguely at the building, "—and doesn't think it's too much. That boy today? He didn't run. That's a good sign."

I wrote in the Good Book that night:

> *Adam visited Rivermead yesterday. Met the residents. Met Kev. Survived what was essentially a group interview with twenty elderly people who have no concept of boundaries.*
>
> *Kev's verdict: decisive approval. He jumped on*

Adam's lap within two minutes and purred for the entire visit. When I tried to get Kev to move so we could have actual privacy, he refused. Stayed right there between us like a furry chaperone who took his duties very seriously.

The residents' verdict: approved. Bert said Adam has "potential."

My verdict: cautiously optimistic. He didn't run when twenty people interrogated him about his intentions. He made Kev purr. He asked about the residents' lives and actually listened to the answers. He brought flowers. He has kind eyes.

Maybe this is what it looks like when things start to go right. Maybe all those disasters were just clearing the path for this. For someone who sees my complicated, exhausting life and says: yes, I'll have that. All of it. Even the interrogation panel.

Also noted: Kev is insufferably smug. Taking full credit.
To be fair, he's earned it.

Denise found me writing and peered over my shoulder. "So? Keeping him?"

"Maybe. If Kev allows it."

"Kev already decided. Didn't you see? That cat practically branded him. Marked him as approved."

"Is that how cats work?"

"That's how this cat works. He's chosen Adam for you. You might as well accept it."

I looked at the Good Book, at all the entries about Kev's visits, his judgments, his uncanny ability to know what people needed. She was right. Kev had decided. And Kev was never wrong. I even accepted Dorothy's appraisement that Michael likely made an out of character decision in the moment.

"Okay," I grinned at Demise. "I accept it."

"Good. Now stop being mushy and come help me with medications. Real work to do."

But she was smiling as she said it, and I was smiling too, and somewhere in the building Kev was probably sleeping off his successful matchmaking session, dreaming smug cat dreams about his latest achievement.

Denise later told everyone. "Dawn's new fella passed the Kev test in under thirty seconds. That's practically a marriage proposal."

I pretended to roll my eyes, but privately, I thought the same.

For weeks afterwards Kev behaved smugly around me, as though personally responsible for my tentative happiness. When Adam sent more flowers, Kev knocked over the vase, but even that felt like approval—an unspoken, *Remember I brought you two together.*

Good Book margin note:

Kev expanding job description to "Therapy cat, inspector of hearts." May require promotion.

* * *

By late July, Adam had become a fixture. Not constantly —he had his own life, his own work—but regularly enough that residents started asking after him. "Where's your young man?" Joyce would inquire. "He was very polite."

He'd come by on weekends sometimes, ostensibly to help with odd jobs (we always had odd jobs), but really just to be around. He'd chat with Arthur about cricket. He'd listen to Dorothy's poems with genuine interest. He'd even earned Bert's grudging approval by correctly identifying a regimental badge in one of Bert's photographs.

"He's not completely useless," Bert declared, which was high praise in Bert-speak.

But it was with Kev that Adam really proved himself.

One Saturday afternoon, Kev appeared unexpectedly—it wasn't a normal day for him to be in, but Mrs. Patterson was at a wedding and Kev had apparently decided the care home was more interesting even at a weekend. He was restless, prowling from room to room with unusual energy.

"Something's up with him," Denise said, frowning. "He's not settling."

Adam, who was helping me sort through donation boxes in the office, looked up. "Maybe he needs to play?"

"Play?"

"Cats need enrichment. Mental stimulation. Especially smart ones." He rummaged in his jacket pocket and pulled out a piece of string from his keyring. "Here, watch."

He dangled the string in front of Kev, who immediately focused with predatory intensity. Adam moved it slowly, letting Kev stalk, then pounce. For ten minutes, they played —Adam patient and attentive, Kev increasingly animated.

By the end, Kev was tired in a good way, the manic energy dissipated. He curled up on the office chair and promptly fell asleep.

"How did you know to do that?" I asked.

"Had cats growing up. They're not that different from difficult teenagers—sometimes they just need to burn off energy." He smiled. "Also, I googled 'how to impress your girlfriend's therapy cat' and string came up a lot."

"Did it also say you're supposed to charm the entire care home?"

"That was improvisation."

We worked side by side, sorting through boxes while Kev snored softly. It was domestic and comfortable and terrifying in how right it felt.

"Dawn?" Adam's voice was careful. "Where do you see this going? Us, I mean."

I stopped, a donated cardigan halfway to the 'keep' pile. "I don't know. I'm not good at relationships. Work always comes first, and that's not fair to—"

"What if I'm okay with that?"

"You say that now—"

"No, listen." He set the box down carefully, his gaze steady. "I'm not asking you to choose. I'm asking if you're willing to try building something that makes room for both. Your work, my work, and... whatever this is between us."

"That sounds complicated." I wasn't trying to push him away, but my heart had to stay grounded, even if it wanted to soar. Too many times before, relationships had crumbled because the man in my life couldn't understand that my heart had space for everyone—that loving others didn't threaten what I felt for him.

"It is complicated," he admitted. "But..." He gestured around the office, to the care home beyond, to Kev dozing in the corner. "This whole thing is complicated, and you make it work. Maybe we could too."

I wanted to argue, to list every reason it might fail. But looking at him—this man who'd spent his Saturday sorting through moth-eaten cardigans and entertaining a cat just to help me—I couldn't.

"Okay," I said softly. "Let's try."

His smile was worth every ounce of fear.

Later, lying in bed, he said: "For the record, Kev called this months ago."

"Called what?"

"Us. That first time I met him, the way he just... decided. Like he knew we'd end up here."

"He's annoyingly perceptive."

"He's a matchmaker. We should get him business cards."

I laughed into his shoulder, feeling something settle in my chest. Not certainty—nothing in life offered that. But hope. The kind that comes from finding someone who sees your complicated, exhausting life and says: yes, I'll have that. All of it.

***

Alicia started working at Rivermead in July, fresh from an agency, twenty-two years old and terrified. She reminded me of myself when I first started—overwhelmed, unsure, but determined to make a difference.

I could see it in the way she held herself, shoulders up around her ears, movements too careful. She smiled constantly—that nervous smile people wear when they're not sure if they're allowed to exist in a space.

"It's a lot to take in," I told her at the end of her first week. "You're doing fine."

"Am I?" She looked unconvinced. "I feel like I'm constantly messing up. Yesterday I couldn't find the right continence pads for Mabel, and I put Florence's compression stockings on wrong, and I—"

"Alicia. You've been here five days. Nobody expects you to know everything yet."

"Claire seems to know everything."

"Claire's been here three years. Give yourself time."

But I could see Alicia struggling. She was good with the technical side—facts. But she was uncomfortable with the intimacy of care work, the way you had to be both professional and deeply personal, maintaining boundaries while also helping someone bathe, dress, use the toilet.

The residents sensed it. Most were patient with her, but a few of the more cantankerous ones—Bert, especially—made their displeasure known.

"That new girl doesn't know what she's doing," Bert complained after Alicia had helped him dress. "Took twenty minutes to do up buttons. Twenty minutes!"

"She's learning, Bert. Everyone has got to learn—"

"Well, she can learn on someone else. I don't want her in my room again."

I talked to Alicia about it, trying to be constructive, but I saw something shutter in her expression. The next day, she called in sick. The day after, she arrived on time but looked like she'd been crying.

"I'm not sure I'm cut out for this," she admitted when I found her in the staff room, staring at her untouched lunch. "I thought I wanted to do care work, but maybe I was wrong. Maybe I should just quit before I really hurt someone."

"You haven't hurt anyone."

"Not yet. But it's only a matter of time, isn't it? I'm so slow, and I get nervous, and then I mess up because I'm nervous, and..." She trailed off, looking miserable.

I was trying to find the right words—something encouraging but honest—when the door opened and Denise poked her head in.

"Dawn? Kev's here, and he's doing something weird."

We followed her to the main lounge where Kev was sitting in the middle of the floor, staring at the corridor that led to the staff areas. Just staring, completely still, his tail swishing back and forth.

"How long's he been like that?" I asked.

"Ten minutes? Won't move. Won't go to any of the residents. Just... sitting there."

As we watched, Kev stood up, walked purposefully down the corridor—past the lounge, past the dining room—and stopped outside the staff room door. He looked back at us and mrowed.

"That's odd," I said.

Kev mrowed again, more insistently.

Alicia, who'd followed us out, stared at him. "Is he... does he want to come in?"

I opened the staff room door. Kev walked in, jumped onto the sofa next to Alicia, and began purring.

"Oh," said Alicia. "Hello?"

Kev climbed into her lap and headbutted her chin.

And then, sitting there with this scruffy ginger cat purring on her knees, Alicia started to cry. Properly cry, all the stress and fear and inadequacy of the past week pouring out while Kev stayed solid and warm and unbothered by her tears.

"I'm sorry," she kept saying. "I'm sorry, I don't know why I'm crying, I just—"

"It's okay," Denise said gently. "Let it out, love."

We left her there, Alicia and Kev, and went back to work. Twenty minutes later, Alicia emerged, red-eyed but calmer, Kev trotting at her heels.

"He's coming with me," she announced. "For my rounds. If that's okay?"

I didn't know how Kev had told her that but that seemed to be Kev's intention and who was I to stand in his way?

"Go ahead," I said.

I watched as Alicia, with Kev beside her, went to help Maureen with afternoon tea. Maureen's face lit up when she saw the cat, and suddenly Alicia wasn't just the nervous new girl—she was the girl who brought Kev. They chatted easily while Alicia helped with the tea, Maureen telling stories about her old cat, Alicia relaxing enough to laugh.

The same thing happened with Dorothy, with Margaret, even with Arthur who normally barely spoke to staff. Kev was a social bridge, an icebreaker, a reason to smile.

When they got to Bert's room, I tensed. This was the test.

"I've brought Kev to visit," Alicia said carefully. "Is that alright?"

Bert looked at her, then at Kev. "The cat can come in. Not sure about you."

"That's fair," Alicia said, and I saw her actually smile—not the nervous smile, but a real one. "I wasn't great with your buttons yesterday. I'll do better next time."

Bert grunted. "See that you do." Then, grudgingly: "Cat seems to like you, though. He's usually a good judge of character."

"High praise," said Alicia, echoing my words from weeks ago.

Kev jumped onto Bert's lap, and Alicia helped him get comfortable in his chair, her movements more confident now, less afraid of getting it wrong.

By the end of her shift, Alicia was a different person. Still learning, still making mistakes, but no longer carrying that terrible weight of inadequacy.

"Thank you," she said to me as she was leaving. "For letting Kev come with me."

"Wasn't my idea. That was all Kev."

She looked at the cat, who was sitting by the French windows, waiting to be let out. "How did he know I needed help?"

"I don't know," I admitted. "But he always seems to."

After that, Alicia flourished. She still did her shifts without Kev, of course—as he was not there all the time—but something had shifted. The residents had accepted her, and she'd found her confidence. Within a month, she was one of our most capable care assistants. Within three, even Bert requested her specifically.

Soon, she was a member of staff and no longer a temp.

"She's not hopeless after all," he told me. "Still slow with buttons, mind you. But she listens. That's rare."

I thought about Kev, about how he'd somehow known that Alicia needed rescuing that day. How he'd chosen her, guided her, given her the boost she needed to keep going.

It was becoming increasingly clear that Kev wasn't just a cat who visited a care home. He was something else entirely. Something we didn't have a name for, but desperately needed.

***

Florence was eighty-nine, sharp as a tack mentally, but bitter. She'd been a solicitor, successful and independent, and she hated being in care. Hated needing help. Hated the loss of control. She was rude to staff, dismissive of other residents, generally unpleasant to be around.

The first time Kev approached her, she waved him away. "I don't like cats. Go away."

Kev sat just out of reach and stared at her.

"I said go away."

Kev yawned.

But something in Kev's calm persistence seemed to intrigue Florence.

"You're not very obedient, are you?" she said.

Kev mrowed.

"Typical cat. Think you own the place." But there was something in her voice—not quite warmth, but not pure hostility either.

Over the next few visits, Kev persisted. He'd sit near Florence, not demanding attention, just... there. Present. Eventually, Florence stopped telling him to go away. Then she stopped pretending to ignore him. Then, one day, I witnessed her reach out and stroke Kev's head.

"You're marginally less irritating than most creatures," Florence informed Kev. I could have sworn then I saw that cat wink at me.

I added to the Good Book:

Florence is officially Team Kev. Never thought I'd see the day. Sometimes the most sceptical people make the best believers once they're converted.

***

Kev had already become something of a local legend. Families began timing their visits to coincide with his rounds, and one devoted daughter even brought her grandchildren solely to catch a glimpse of "the famous cat." His growing reputation even caught the attention of the local Gazette, who called to inquire about "our therapy animal initiative." Kev, however, remained unimpressed. He considered the reporter for a moment, yawned dramatically, and retreated under a chair. The interview was officially declined. His fame, it seemed, would stay local—and entirely on his own terms.

Meanwhile, Millie was preparing for a milestone of her own. On the third of July, she turned one hundred. She greeted the occasion with characteristic nonchalance. "Been a long century," she remarked with a shrug in her broad Yorkshire accent. "Might as well have cake." (A sentiment that endeared her to Denise, who shared her practical outlook.)

Over breakfast, she announced with a mischievous twinkle in her eye, "Hundred today. Don't feel a day over ninety-nine."

The day itself was quintessential high summer. The garden paths had baked dry under the sun, and the roses stood at their peak—heavy-headed and fragrant, their scent drifting on the warm air. It was the kind of July day that seemed to stretch endlessly, bathed in golden light under a cloudless blue sky.

We'd planned a modest celebration for Millie at 3 PM, complete with balloons, a Victoria sponge cake, and the mayor's and Queen's congratulatory card. When I asked her what she wanted most for her birthday, she didn't hesitate. "To give Kev a cuddle," she said with a twinkle in her eye.

True to form, Kev obliged—proving once again that he was not just a local celebrity, but a cherished companion.

At three o'clock, he'd strolled into the lounge as if on cue. Millie clapped her hands, delighted. "He's punctual! I like that."

Kev jumped onto her lap with surprising gentleness. He sniffed her cardigan, then settled.

"Oh, he's warm," Millie murmured, stroking his fur.

She traced the rough patch on his ear. "I had one just like you when my father worked down the mines," she said. "He'd sit beside me while I waited for him to come home, purring as if to say everything would be all right. I used to think that if the cat wasn't afraid, maybe I didn't need to be either."

Her voice softened. "Funny, isn't it, how a bit of fur can keep you brave."

Everyone laughed. Millie went on reminiscing, voice gaining strength. "People think reaching a hundred is about luck. It's not. It's about having something—or someone—to care for, even when it hurts."

Kev purred louder.

The party went on around them—laughter, music, Victoria sponge cake—but Millie seemed to inhabit a quieter bubble, humming softly to the rhythm of Kev's purrs. At one point she looked up and caught my eye.

"Promise me," she said, "you'll let him keep doing his rounds. Even after I've gone. Everyone needs something warm to love."

"He will," I said.

She nodded, satisfied. "Good. No one should have to grow old without a cat."

When we brought out the cake, she insisted Kev have the first sniff. He obliged, then sneezed dramatically, which set the whole room laughing.

Before she went to bed, Millie patted my hand. "It was a good day," she said. "When you're my age, a good day's better than a good year."

I believed her.

I wrote later:

July 3rd: Millie's 100th birthday.. Kev sat on her lap through the whole celebration She said life isn't measured in years but in creatures we've loved. I wrote that down twice.

***

It's difficult to recall what Rivermead was like before Kev. He had become so deeply ingrained in our daily lives over six months that newcomers often assumed he was a permanent fixture of the building. For those of us who'd been there longer, he was something even more profound—a quiet testament to the fact that kindness doesn't always need to be loud or dramatic. Sometimes, it's as simple as a comforting presence, a gentle weight in your lap when you need a reminder that you're still here, still seen.

It happened on a sticky, humid afternoon in mid-July. Kev was on his usual rounds—he'd just finished visiting Arthur and was heading toward Grace—when he hopped down from a chair and landed awkwardly. His right front paw gave a slight wobble, and he let out a sharp *mrow* that sounded more startled than pained. But then he lifted the paw and refused to put any weight on it.

The lounge fell silent, the air suddenly heavy with concern.

"Kev?" Maureen's voice cut through the stillness, tight with unease.

"Something's wrong," Dorothy said, voicing what everyone was already thinking.

By the time I got there—summoned by three separate staff members in under thirty seconds—the lounge was in chaos. Grace was in tears, Bert was swearing under his breath, and Maureen, despite her arthritic knees, had lowered herself to the floor to examine Kev's paw. He sat patiently, though his expression was one of mild confusion as she fumbled to inspect him.

"Let me see," I said, crouching beside him. I gently lifted the injured paw. He didn't resist or pull away, which worried me more than if he'd hissed or swatted.

There was no obvious sign of injury—no blood, no swelling, nothing to explain why he refused to put weight on it. But something was clearly wrong.

"Alright," I said, trying to keep my voice steady even as my heart pounded. "I'm taking him to the vet. Denise, can you grab his carrier?"

She was already there, carrier in one hand and car keys in the other. "Got it," she said firmly. "I'm driving. You're too stressed."

She wasn't wrong. My hands trembled as I tried to coax Kev into the carrier. He went in reluctantly, shooting me a look that unmistakably communicated: *This is beneath me, and I'm not pleased about it.*

By the time we left, the mood in the building had shifted entirely. Three residents were openly crying, Bert had retreated to his room—a telltale sign he was deeply upset—and the staff huddled together in anxious groups, their faces etched with worry.

"He'll be fine," I assured them, forcing a confidence I didn't quite feel. "It's probably just a sprain."

"Call us the *second* you know anything," Claire insisted, her voice tight with concern.

The drive to the vet was only fifteen minutes, but it felt like an eternity. Kev let out occasional meows from his carrier—not his usual bold, commanding *mrow*, but softer, more tentative sounds that twisted like a knife in my chest.

"He's going to be fine," Denise said firmly, though her white-knuckled grip on the steering wheel betrayed her own anxiety. "He's Kev. He's indestructible."

"Nothing's indestructible," I muttered, while dialling the vets to let them know we were en-route.

"He is," Denise shot back, her tone unwavering. "He made it through life as a stray, who knows what kind of hell he faced before that. A sprained paw isn't going to take him out."

I wanted to believe her. But I couldn't shake the memory of the way he'd looked at me in the lounge—confused, hurt, like he couldn't understand why his body was betraying him. And then there were the residents, how much they adored him, how shattered they'd be if something was seriously wrong.

The vet's office was mercifully quiet when we arrived. Dr. Morrison appeared within minutes—she'd treated Kev before and knew his story, his importance to Rivermead. She also knew the arrangement we had with Mrs. Patterson: if she was tied up or it was an emergency, we had the green light to bring Kev in and make decisions. 'Joint custody' as Mrs P put it, even though in truth Kev's was more often at ours now than hers.

I wondered often whether we were the 'something else' Mrs P had mentioned she thought Kev was looking for. And then I began to muse on why he hadn't come to us before and whether he'd been waiting for us—or more specifically me—to be ready for him. It took me when I was at my lowest to say yes.

"What happened?" the vet asked, already opening the carrier.

"He jumped and landed wrong. Won't put any weight on his right front paw."

She lifted Kev out carefully and set him on the examination table. He sat there, looking smaller and more uncertain than I'd ever seen him, a far cry from his usual commanding presence. It made my chest ache just to see him like that.

"Let's take a look, Kev," she said, her voice calm and reassuring. She ran her hands over him methodically, professional yet gentle. When she reached the injured paw, Kev flinched slightly but didn't pull away.

She manipulated it carefully, checking for breaks and testing its range of motion. Kev endured it all with the stoicism of someone who'd weathered far worse.

Finally, she sat back. "Good news—nothing's broken. No tears that I can feel. It looks like a sprain, likely from landing awkwardly. He'll need some rest and anti-inflammatory medication, but he should be back to normal in a few days."

I felt my legs go weak with relief. "That's it? Just a sprain?"

"Just a sprain. Though at his age—he's what, eight?—he needs to be more careful. Cats start losing some of their agility as they get older. That jump might have been routine a year ago, but now..." She shrugged. "Bodies change."

"So what do we do?"

"Rest, medication, no jumping for at least a week. After that, he should be back to normal. But Dawn—" she looked at me seriously, "—this is a reminder. He's not young anymore. He's middle-aged for a cat. You need to start thinking about that."

"I know. I will. Thank you."

She prescribed the medication, gave me detailed instructions, and sent us on our way with Kev back in his carrier, dignity somewhat restored by the promise that he wasn't dying.

On the drive back, I called the home. Claire answered before the first ring finished.

"Well?"

"Sprained paw. He's fine. Needs rest but he's fine."

I heard her relay this to the room, heard the collective exhale, the relieved voices.

"Thank God," Claire said. "Bert's been in his room for the last hour. Won't come out. Grace has been crying. Maureen's already made him a get-well card."

"Tell them we're on our way back and all is well."

When we arrived, the reception felt like something from a medical drama. Residents lined the corridor. Staff clustered by the door. Even Florence—Florence who claimed to barely tolerate Kev—was there, wringing her hands.

I opened the carrier. Kev emerged slowly, still favouring one paw but looking more annoyed than injured. He surveyed his welcoming committee with what I can only describe as embarrassment.

"He's fine," I announced. "Just a sprain. Needs to rest for

a few days, but he's fine."

The relief was palpable. Maureen started crying again—happy tears this time. Grace clasped her hands together. Arthur let out a breath he'd been holding.

And then, as if choreographed, they all started fussing.

Maureen had already made a card—complete with drawings of cats and get-well messages in three different colours of marker. Grace had contributed a poem she'd painstakingly written out, only stumbling over a few words. Arthur had saved the cream from his afternoon tea "in case Kev needed building up."

Someone—I suspect Denise—had set up a cushioned bed in the corner of the lounge, piled with soft blankets. Kev was ceremoniously carried to it like a king on a sedan (he tolerated this with remarkable patience) and settled in like a small orange potentate.

For the next two days, he held court from his cushioned throne: Mrs P agreeing it would be best if he stayed with us rather than bringing him back and forth or him trying to walk. Residents would come sit beside him, bringing treats (approved by me first), reading to him, telling him stories. Staff would check on him between tasks. Even Bert emerged from his room to sit with Kev for an hour, reading the paper aloud in his gruff voice.

"Don't do that again," I heard him mutter at one point. "Scared the hell out of us, you daft sod."

Kev mrowed softly, as if apologising.

The limping became somewhat theatrical by day two. I'd watch him walk relatively normally when he thought no one was looking, then resume the pathetic hobble when residents appeared with treats.

"Hypochondriac," Denise muttered, watching him milk the sympathy.

"Smart cat," I corrected. "Why walk when you can be carried? Why hunt for treats when they come to you?"

But even I had to admit he was pushing it. By day three, when Margaret arrived with yet another offering of chicken, Kev limped toward her with the dedication of a method actor, stopping halfway to look back and make sure everyone was watching his suffering.

"You're fine," I told him. "The vet said you're fine. Stop performing."

He gave me a look of profound betrayal and limped onward. Margaret cooed sympathetically.

A few days later, he was walking properly again, though he still accepted the extra attention with regal grace. The cushioned bed remained, had become "Kev's chair," and he'd use it whenever he wanted to nap in the lounge.

But the incident had shaken us all. For those fifteen minutes between him limping and us knowing it was just a sprain, we'd all faced the possibility of losing him. And it had been terrifying.

That evening, I found Bert in his room again, staring at the photograph of Kev that now sat on his bedside table—one I'd taken months ago of the two of them together.

"You alright, Bert?"

"Thought we were losing him. When he couldn't walk properly. Thought that was it."

"Just a sprain."

"This time. But he's getting older, isn't he?" Bert's voice was rough. "I'm eighty-seven. I know what getting older means. Things stop working the way they should. Bodies give out. And he's not a young cat anymore."

"He's middle-aged. That's not old."

"It's not young either." Bert was quiet for a moment. "I don't know how much time I've got left. And now I'm wondering—how much time does he have? Will I outlive him? Or will he outlive me? And which is worse?"

I didn't have an answer for that. Both options seemed unbearable in different ways.

"Let's not worry about that now," I said finally. "He's fine. You're fine. We'll take it one day at a time."

"That's all we can ever do, isn't it?" Bert said. "One day at a time. But it doesn't make it less frightening."

I wrote in the Good Book that night:

Kev injured his paw. Just a sprain, nothing serious, but for that half an hour or so before we knew—the fear in that building was palpable. Three residents cried. Bert hid in his room. Everyone stopped what they were doing and waited.

It made me realise something I'd been avoiding: Kev won't be here forever. He's about eight years old—middle-aged for a cat. The vet reminded me of that today. Bodies change. He's not as agile as he was. He needs to be more careful.

And if a sprained paw can cause this much fear, what happens when something serious goes wrong? Because something will, eventually. That's the deal we made when we let him into our lives. We borrowed him from time, knowing we'd have to give him back. Pets never do live long enough.

The residents have showered him with attention these past few days. Cards, treats, poems, company. He milked it shamelessly, limping theatrically whenever an audience appeared. By day three he was practically performing Shakespearean death scenes for extra chicken.

But underneath the comedy, there's something serious: we all love him more than we've admitted, even to ourselves. And love means vulnerability. Means risk. Means accepting that someday—maybe soon, maybe later, but someday—we're going to have to say goodbye.

Not today, though. Today he's fine. Today he's getting spoiled rotten and accepting it as his due. Today is enough.

The incident changed something, though. Made us all more aware. More careful. We stopped encouraging him to jump onto high surfaces. Started making sure he had easier access to his favourite spots. Watched him more closely for signs of pain or stiffness.

And we loved him more fiercely, knowing now—really knowing—that our time with him was finite.

"We're being ridiculous," I told Denise, watching three residents fuss over Kev like anxious parents.

"We're being human," she corrected. "We love him. We nearly lost him (in our heads). Now we're overcompensating. It's normal."

"Is it helping?"

"Probably not. But it makes us feel better, and that counts for something."

She was right. And Kev, to his credit, tolerated the extra attention with his usual grace. He seemed to understand that we needed this—needed to feel like we were protecting him, even though he'd been protecting us all along.

Good Book:

Cat recovered in forty-eight hours. Emotional recovery of staff ongoing.

* * *

Adam, still carrying that easy laugh Kev approved, was making regular stops at Rivermead, bringing pastries and other treats in for the staff.

Denise couldn't stop gushing. "A man who shows up with cake without being asked," she'd say, "is the sweetest thing." Then, with a mischievous pause, she'd add, "If you're ever done with him, Dawn, send him my way." She'd follow it up with a wink, fully aware my response would be an indignant, "Get lost."

Adam had a way of slipping into the rhythm of our days as if he'd always belonged. Tea, cake, the hum of conversation, even the stray cat hair clinging to his jumper—Kev treated him like part of the furniture, which, in our world, was the ultimate stamp of approval.

It was the sort of settled, easy routine that made the sudden arrival of med students all the more noticeable. Every so often, the university would send a fresh batch for their community placement. Some were earnest and eager, others merely ticking boxes until they could move on to the next module. But regardless of their attitude, they all shared one thing: that deer-in-the-headlights look, terrified of making a mistake.

This year's cohort arrived in the thick of summer—four wide-eyed twenty-somethings clutching folders like lifelines. They did their best to look professional, but you could see it in their faces: they were drowning in the reality of geriatric care, silently longing for the sun-soaked beaches of Ibiza instead.

I gave them the usual tour, the usual speech about dignity and person-centred care, the usual warnings about bodily fluids and difficult behaviours. They nodded earnestly, made notes, asked polite questions.

Then we got to the lounge where Kev was holding court, surrounded by admirers.

"And that's Kev," I said. "Our therapy cat."

One of the students, Maya, lit up. "Oh my god, you have a therapy cat? That's amazing! Can I pet him?"

"If he lets you."

The students clustered around Kev, who accepted their adoration with regal patience. But I noticed him watching one student in particular: a quiet girl named Zainab who hung back from the group, not participating in the cooing and petting.

After a few minutes, Kev extracted himself from his admirers and walked directly to Zainab. He sat at her feet and stared up at her.

"He wants you to pet him," Maya called over.

"I'm okay," Zainab said quietly.

"Are you allergic?" I asked.

"No. I just... I'm not really a cat person."

Kev continued staring. Zainab looked uncomfortable.

"You don't have to," I assured her. "Kev won't be offended."

But Kev stayed put, and Zainab's discomfort grew. Finally, she bent down and gave him one perfunctory pat on the head.

Kev immediately wound around her legs, purring.

"He likes you," I said.

"Great." Zainab's tone suggested this was anything but great.

Over the following weeks, I watched Zainab struggle, like Alicia had, with the emotional aspects of care. She kept everyone at arm's length: residents, staff, even her fellow students.

When Florence asked about her day, Zainab gave clipped, minimal responses. When Maureen tried to show her photographs, Zainab found reasons to be elsewhere. She did her job, but it was clear she was counting down the hours until she could leave.

"She's not cut out for this," Denise said after week two. "Too cold. Care work requires heart."

But I'd noticed something: Kev sought Zainab out every visit. Would sit beside her during handover, follow her on her rounds, insert himself between her and whatever task she was performing.

And Zainab, despite her protests that she wasn't a cat person, would absently pet him while charting or talking to residents. Her voice would soften slightly when he was there. Her shoulders would drop from their defensive hunch.

One day, I found Zainab in the garden, sitting on a bench, crying silently. Kev was on her lap.

I almost left—this felt private—but something stopped me.

"Zainab? You okay?"

She wiped her face roughly. "Fine. I just needed some air."

I sat down beside her, not too close. "Rough day?"

"They're all rough days." She laughed bitterly. "I don't know why I'm doing this course. I'm clearly terrible at it."

"You're not terrible. Your clinical skills are excellent."

And they were from what I had seen.

"But I can't... I can't do the other stuff. The chatting, the caring about their grandchildren, the pretending I'm interested in stories about the war. I just..." She broke down properly now. "I just feel nothing. And that makes me a monster, doesn't it?"

I was going to say 'No, it doesn't', but as I stared down at Kev, I decided on a different tack. "Why do you think you feel nothing?"

"Because my gran died in a place like this - just before Covid. And it was awful. She was lonely and forgotten and the staff were overworked and the place smelled of piss and despair, and I watched her just... fade away. Die slowly while everyone around her was dying slowly too. And I promised myself I'd never work in care, never be part of that system."

She looked at me with red eyes. "But then I got here and it's not like that. You actually care. The staff care. Even this bloody cat cares. And it's making me feel things I don't want to feel, remember things I'd rather forget."

Kev, still on her lap, increased his purring.

"Zainab," I said gently, "grief doesn't make you a monster. And neither does being scared of caring."

"I'm not scared—"

"You are. You're bloody terrified. Because if you let yourself care about these residents, if you let them in, then you'll hurt when they die. Like you hurt when your gran died. And you're trying to protect yourself by keeping everyone at a distance."

She was crying harder now. "It hurts so much. Missing

her. And seeing all these elderly people here, knowing they're all going to die too, knowing their families will hurt like I hurt... I can't bear it."

"So you shut down."

"Yes."

Kev stood up on her lap, balancing carefully, and headbutted her chin. Then he climbed onto her shoulder like an orange scarf on top of her hijab and pressed his face against her neck.

Zainab lost it completely, sobbing into Kev's fur while he purred steadily against her throat.

I let her cry. Sometimes that's all you can do.

When she finally quieted, I said, "Your gran's care home —did it have a Kev?"

"What?"

"Someone or something that brought joy. That made the difficult days bearable. That reminded everyone why they were there."

Zainab thought about it. "No. Nothing like that. It was just... institutional. Efficient but empty."

"That's what we're trying not to be. But it only works if the staff care. If they let themselves be affected by the residents, form connections, risking the grief." I paused. "You have two choices: shut down completely and become technically competent but emotionally absent, or open yourself up and risk the hurt but gain something beautiful in return."

"What if I can't? What if I'm too damaged?"

"Then Kev wasted his time on you, and he never wastes time."

She laughed, watery but genuine. "He is persistent, isn't he?"

"Very. And he sees something in you worth persisting for."

Zainab stayed for the rest of her placement. She didn't

transform overnight—healing doesn't work that way—but gradually she softened. Started listening to the residents' stories. Started caring despite herself.

On her last day, she brought a card for me and a laser light pointer for Kev.

"Thank you," she said. "For not giving up on me. And for showing me that care homes don't have to be like the one my gran was in."

"What will you do now? What path are you going to follow?"

"Geriatrics," she said firmly. "I'm going to specialise in elderly care. Make sure there are more places like this and fewer like..." She didn't finish, but I understood.

After she left, I found Denise in the staff room. "You were right," I told her. "Zainab wasn't cut out for this."

"Told you."

"She's better than us. She's going to be extraordinary."

Denise looked at me, confused.

"She nearly broke from grief," I explained. "Shut down completely to protect herself. But she chose to feel anyway. Chose to risk the hurt. That takes more courage than coming to this work naturally caring."

I updated the Good Book:

Student doctor Zainab *finished her placement today. Started as one of the most emotionally distant students we've ever had; ended as one of the most promising.*

Kev knew, of course. Knew she wasn't cold—just wounded. Knew that sometimes the people who resist caring the most are the ones who will care the deepest once they let themselves.

Note to self: trust the cat's judgment, even when—especially when—it contradicts your own.

* * *

Not all of Kev's work happened during official visiting

hours.

It was a Monday night in late July when I got the call. I was at home, already in my pyjamas, about to go to bed. The night shift supervisor, a capable woman named Ruth, sounded stressed.

"Dawn, I'm so sorry to call, but we have a situation. It's Agnes in room eight. She's very distressed, and nothing we're doing is helping. She's asking for her son—he died five years ago—and she's getting quite agitated. I'm worried she might hurt herself or one of the staff."

Agnes was ninety-one, with advanced dementia. She'd been with us for just a few days after transferring from another home, and we'd been forewarned she had episodes like this occasionally—sundowning, the doctors called it, when dementia symptoms worsened in the evening.

"Have you tried—" I started to run through the usual checklist.

"We've tried everything," Ruth interrupted. "Music, warm milk, gentle redirection. She's beyond that now. I'm about to call the doctor for emergency medication, but I thought I'd check with you first."

I was already getting dressed. "I'll be there in fifteen minutes. Don't sedate her yet unless you absolutely have to."

I drove through empty streets, trying to think. I'd been told by her previous carers that Agnes's agitation episodes usually passed if we could just ride them out, but they were hard on her and hard on staff. Sedation was a last resort—it made her foggy for days afterward.

When I arrived, I could hear Agnes before I saw her. She was in the corridor, walking back and forth, wringing her hands, calling for her son in increasing desperation.

"Joseph! Where's Joseph? He should be here. Why isn't he here?"

Two care assistants were flanking her, trying to provide calm presence without crowding her, but Agnes was deteriorating. Her breath was coming in gasps. She was starting to scratch at her own arms, a self-soothing behaviour that would leave marks.

"Agnes," I said gently, approaching slowly. "I'm Dawn. Can I help you find what you need?"

"Joe!" She looked at me but didn't see me. "Where's my boy? He should be back from school!"

I was about to try another tactic when I heard it: a thump from the office window, then a mrow.

Kev. He must have been sleeping in the office and heard the commotion.

"Can someone let the cat in?" I said.

Ruth nodded to one of the care assistants. A moment later, Kev appeared in the corridor.

He took one look at Agnes and walked directly to her.

Agnes stopped pacing. "A cat?"

"That's Kev," I said softly. "He lives here when he feels like it. Would you like to say hello?"

Kev sat at Agnes's feet and looked up at her with those calm amber eyes.

"Hello, cat," Agnes said, her voice already quieter.

Kev stood and rubbed against her legs. Agnes's hands, which had been fluttering anxiously, lowered to touch his head.

"Would you like to sit down with him?" I gestured to a nearby chair.

Agnes let herself be guided to the chair. Kev immediately jumped into her lap—something he usually reserved for residents he knew well—and began purring loudly.

Agnes's breathing slowed. Her shoulders dropped. The desperate, seeking look left her eyes.

"We had a cat," she said, stroking Kev. "When Joe was small. An orange one like this. Joe loved that cat. They say gingers are the most affectionate."

"That sounds nice," I said, sitting nearby.

Kev, the Care Home Cat

"He'd carry it everywhere. The cat was so patient with him." She smiled, lost in the memory. "I don't remember its name anymore. Isn't that silly? Can't remember our own cat's name."

"It's not silly."

We sat like that for twenty minutes,

Agnes petting Kev, talking about her son as a child, about the life she'd had before dementia stole it. The agitation didn't return. Eventually, she was calm enough to be guided back to her room, where Kev stayed with her until she fell asleep.

Ruth found me in the corridor afterward, looking shaken. "I've never seen anything like that. She was heading toward a full crisis, and that cat just... fixed it."

"He has a gift," I said simply.

After that night, staff started calling Kev whenever there was a difficult situation. Someone agitated? Get Kev. Someone in pain? See if Kev will visit. Someone just had bad news from family? Kev might help.

He didn't always come—he had his own schedule, his own priorities—doing what cats do at night—but when he did, he almost always made things better.

And so often, he would appear just as we realised we needed him, as if we'd sent out a psychic text into the cosmos in cat language—and he'd read it.

I added a section to the Good Book:

Agnes, sundowning. Kev appeared and within minutes had calmed a situation that was heading toward crisis. He stayed with her until she slept. The staff are starting to see him as a colleague, not just a visitor. Maybe that's what he's always been.

***

It was Denise's idea to throw a 'proper' summer garden party, and she was determined to make it happen.

The late July heat shimmered off the patio, and the garden was at its most glorious—everything in full bloom at once, the air heavy with the scent of roses, lavender, and freshly cut grass. It was the perfect setting, she insisted, for something elegant and memorable.

"Like the ones posh people have," she said, gesturing with her tea mug in the staff room, anything but poshly. "Hats, finger sandwiches, Pimm's if we can get away with it, and slightly undercooked sausages because, let's face it, nobody actually knows how barbecues work."

"We can't serve alcohol to the residents," I reminded her, leaning against the counter, smiling at the idea nonetheless of a few of them getting tipsy.

"Non-alcoholic Pimm's exists," she shot back, grinning. "I checked. We can do this properly."

It was only then that I realised she'd been planning this for weeks. She pulled out a list—an *actual* list—complete with bullet points, a budget breakdown, and even a rain contingency plan.

"When did you have time to plan all this?" I asked, flipping through the pages.

"Night shifts," she said with a shrug. "What else am I supposed to do at three a.m.? Anyway, it's perfect. An end-of-summer celebration. Something for everyone to look forward to. The residents need it—they've been cooped up through that awful rainy spell. *We* need it. And..." She paused, her tone shifting slightly, "it would be a good chance for Adam to meet everyone properly. Not just the interrogation panel."

Her words lingered in the air, and I could see the unspoken meaning behind them. This wasn't just about a garden party—it was about connection, about creating a moment that mattered. And, as usual, Denise had already thought of everything.

"He's already met everyone."

"He met them in interview mode. This is different. This is him seeing you at work. Seeing how you are with them. Seeing if he can handle your actual life, not just the sanitised version."

She had a point, much as I hated to admit it.

"And he can bring more cake."

"Fine. But if this turns into a disaster—"

"It won't. Trust me. I'm excellent at parties."

The planning consumed the next two weeks. Residents got involved immediately—it gave them purpose, something to contribute. Dorothy, Joyce and Maureen formed a decorations committee, spending hours making bunting from old magazines and fabric scraps. Arthur appointed himself chief quality controller, testing various sandwich fillings and declaring most of them "acceptable with reservations."

Bert, predictably, appointed himself head of the beer tent (non-alcoholic beer, after much negotiation) and took the role with military seriousness.

"Can't have people serving themselves willy-nilly," he announced. "Need proper portion control. Organisation. Discipline."

"It's elderflower cordial, Bert, not the Normandy landings."

"Proper planning prevents poor performance. That's what we said in the army."

Grace volunteered to help with invitations, painstakingly writing out names in her improving handwriting, only occasionally needing help with words. Each finished invitation was a small victory.

Even Florence got involved, offering to coordinate the music selection. "Nothing after 1970" she declared. "And no Andrew Lloyd Webber. I have standards."

When I mentioned it to Adam, his response was immediate: "I'll help. What do you need?"

"You don't have to—"

"I want to. What's the point of dating someone if I can't help at their care home garden party? Besides, I flip a mean burger."

"Do you actually?"

"No idea. But how hard can it be?"

The morning of the party, I arrived to find Denise already there with Claire, setting up tables in the garden.

"Couldn't sleep," Denise admitted. "Too excited. This is going to be brilliant."

By noon, everything was in place. Tables covered in mismatched cloths (donated by various families). Bunting strung between trees. A borrowed gazebo in case of rain, although the weather was just right today - not too hot and not too cold, proving once more the weather gods were being kind. The barbecue—intimidating and mysterious—set up by the patio. Bert's beer tent (a folding table with a sign) positioned with military precision.

The air smelled of charcoal smoke and sausages, cut grass and roses. Someone had strung fairy lights through the trees even though it was still daylight—and I knew they'd look magical later.

Adam arrived at one, with more flowers for the staff room—an instant win—and sleeves rolled up ready for the barbecue, earning approving looks from Denise within minutes.

"Finally," she whispered to me, "someone under fifty who knows how to use tongs."

He nodded towards the bags he'd brought. "Reinforcements," he announced. "Extra bread rolls, emergency cake," Denise nodded her approval. "And—" he pulled out a small bag, "—cat treats. Figured Kev would show up."

"It's Saturday. Not his usual day." I said.

"He'll show up. Cats know when there's food involved.

Like Denise when the cake's out."

Denise grinned, midway through wiping a crumb off her lip. Adam knew her already.

The residents started gathering at two. Most were in their best—Maureen wore a hat with flowers, Arthur had put on a tie, Joyce had her pearls. Even Bert had made an effort, wearing his best blazer.

Janet arrived with Tom, having one of her clearer days. She took in the decorations with delight. "It's like a real garden party. Like the ones we used to go to."

"It is a real garden party," Tom assured her.

"Is it? Good. I like garden parties."

By half past two, the garden was full of residents, families who'd come to visit, staff taking their breaks. The barbecue was smoking (literally—Adam was discovering that flipping burgers was indeed quite hard), music was playing (Ella Fitzgerald, Florence-approved), and the atmosphere was exactly what we'd hoped for: festive, relaxed, happy.

And then Kev appeared.

He materialised at the garden gate like visiting royalty, surveying the scene with obvious approval. The residents spotted him immediately.

"Kev!"

"He came!"

"Someone get him some cream from the cream tea!"

He sauntered down the path like visiting royalty, tail high, accepting greetings and pets from his admirers. When he reached Adam—still valiantly wrestling with the barbecue—he sat down and stared.

"Hello, mate," Adam said, wiping sweat from his forehead. "Come to supervise?"

Kev mrowed.

"Thought so. How am I doing?"

Kev sniffed the air, considered, then rubbed against Adam's leg. Approval granted.

"Thank God. The cat thinks I'm competent. That's something."

I watched them from across the garden—Adam crouched down, scratching Kev's ears while explaining his burger-flipping strategy, Kev listening with the patience of someone humouring a student. Something in my chest went warm and soft.

"He's a keeper," Maureen said beside me, making me jump.

"Sorry?"

"Adam. He's good with the residents. Good with you. And most importantly—" she nodded toward where Kev was now sprawled on the grass beside the barbecue, supervising, "—good with our boy. That's the real test, isn't it?"

"I suppose it is."

"And he passed. Kev wouldn't lie there if he wasn't comfortable. He'd have moved off to somewhere quieter. But he's staying close. That means something."

She was right. Kev stayed near Adam for most of the afternoon—sometimes beside the barbecue, sometimes under the table where Adam was sitting, sometimes on his lap when Adam finally abandoned the cooking to someone more competent.

I watched Adam navigate the afternoon with remarkable grace. He fetched tea for residents without being asked. Helped Grace cut her burger when she was struggling with the knife. Sat with Bert and admired his beer-tent organisation. Even got Margaret's pigeon-chasing story for the third time and laughed like it was the first.

At one point, he and Tom ended up in conversation about teaching, about students and patience and trying to reach people who don't necessarily want to be reached.

"It's not that different," Adam said, gesturing with his tea. "Whether you're teaching Year 10s or caring for people with dementia. It's about meeting them where they are. Not where you think they should be."

Tom looked at him with something like respect. "Most people don't understand that. They think care is about fixing people, making them normal again. But sometimes care is just about being present. Bearing witness."

"Exactly."

I found myself blinking back tears. There he was—this man I'd known for barely three months—talking about care work like he understood it. Like he understood me.

Later, as we were packing up (residents inside, staff cleaning), Adam found me by the gazebo, folding tablecloths.

"You're amazing at this, you know," he said.

"At folding tablecloths?"

"At running a village fête, yes. But also at making a whole place feel like home. Watching you today—the way you know everyone's names, their preferences, their stories. The way they light up when you talk to them. It's remarkable."

"It's just the job."

"It's not, though. Not everyone could do what you do. Not everyone would want to." He took the tablecloth from my hands, set it aside, pulled me close. "I'm proud of you. I know I haven't earned the right to say that yet, but I am. Proud and impressed and slightly intimidated by your competence."

"Slightly?"

"Very. You're terrifying when you're in charge."

I laughed against his shoulder, feeling the day's tension drain away. "Did you have fun?"

"Loved it. Your residents are brilliant. Bert taught me about proper beverage rationing. Dorothy gave me a reading list. Grace wrote me a poem—it's mostly swear words, but it rhymes. And Kev—" he looked down, where Kev had appeared again and was figure-eighting between our legs,

"—Kev has decided I'm still acceptable."

"High praise."

"The highest. I take it very seriously."

We stood there in the fading afternoon light, Kev purring at our feet, the garden soft and quiet after the chaos.

"I love you," Adam said suddenly. "I know it's early and maybe I shouldn't say it yet, but I do. I love you and your impossible job and your elderly family and your supervisor cat. All of it."

My throat went tight. "I love you too."

"Yeah?"

"Yeah. Even though you're terrible at barbecuing." I kissed his cheek.

"Hey, I got better. Toward the end there was only minimal charring."

Kev mrowed loudly, as if agreeing or protesting—hard to tell which.

"The cat agrees with me," I said.

"The cat is biased. I gave him treats."

"Smart cat."

We kissed, and Kev made a disgusted sound and stalked off toward the building, tail high, leaving us to our moment.

That night, I wrote in the Good Book:

Garden party a success. No injuries, minimal chaos, only one fire alarm (barbecue-related). Residents happy. Staff happy. Kev spent the afternoon supervising and approving.

Adam was wonderful. Natural with residents, patient with their stories, good with Kev. Rubbish at barbecuing. Watched him navigate my world and thought: yes, this could work. This might actually work.

Sometimes happiness sneaks up on you. You're so used to things being hard that you miss the moment when they become easy. When someone fits into your life like they were always meant to be there. Like they're home.

Denise found me writing and read over my shoulder

without shame.

"Told you the party was a good idea."

"You were right."

"Say it again. I want to savour you saying, 'Denise, you were right.'"

"Denise, you were right. The party was perfect. Happy?"

"Ecstatic. Now admit the other thing."

"What other thing?"

"That Kev's matchmaking services are infallible. That you should have trusted him from the start. That I was right about that too."

I looked at Kev, who'd returned and was sprawled across my desk like he owned it. He opened one eye, gave me that slow, smug blink.

"Fine. Denise, you were right about that too. Kev was right. Are you happy now?"

"Delighted. Though Kev's the one taking credit. Look at him. He's practically preening."

She was right. Kev looked insufferably pleased with himself. As he should. He'd vetted Adam thoroughly, given his approval, and been proven correct. Again.

"Thank you," I told him, scratching behind his ears.

He purred, accepting his due.

After all, matchmaking was just another form of therapy. And Kev was very, very good at his job.

***

The weather shifted abruptly from glorious sunshine to relentless rain, and the final week of August was consumed by it—cold, unyielding, and ceaseless. It was that kind of August Bank Holiday rain that feels like summer surrendering, not yet cold but the damp stubbornly persistent. The kind that makes you forget there was ever sunshine, that there will ever be sunshine again.

The sound of the rain tapping against the windows was a

constant backdrop. The garden turned to mud, tempers shortened, and even Kev looking out of the conservatory at the drenched garden looked offended.

By Thursday, the mood had sunk to its lowest point, so I decided to bring in a box of writing paper and coloured pens.

"Let's write letters," I suggested. "To anyone you like—past or present. No rules."

At first, there were groans. "What's the point?" Bert grumbled. "Everyone I'd write to is dead."

"Then they're guaranteed to read it quietly," I replied.

That earned a snort.

Kev leapt onto the table, scattering envelopes, and sat squarely in the middle.

"See?" I told them. "Editorial supervision."

That got a laugh, and soon everyone was scribbling. Dorothy began to write a poem, a sonnet "to the only man I've ever trusted—who happens to have four legs." Grace, concentrating hard, whispered each word aloud as she formed it, wrote simply, "Dear world, I am still here." Arthur wrote to his late wife, telling her about "our new ginger staff member."

Bert took the longest. When he finished, he folded his single sheet carefully and sealed it in an envelope addressed simply: *To whoever finds this later.*

When we were done, the table was strewn with envelopes, marked by the faint circles of teacups and the inky paw prints left by Kev as he wandered over Dorothy's elegant blue fountain pen script.

"Should we post them?" Alicia asked.

"Some will be delivered," I said. "Some already reached who they're meant for."

Kev pawed at one envelope until it fell onto the floor. It was from Bert, addressed to "Whoever reads this after I've gone."

I picked it up and looked at Bert and his eyes said 'Go on, read it.'

Inside he'd written, in his blunt script:

To whoever finds this after I've gone,

Don't let the quiet spook you. It's just the world taking a moment to breathe. I spent most of my life dodging silence—always had the radio on, the telly in the background, anything to keep my thoughts at bay. But when you get to my age, and everyone you've loved has either passed on or moved away, the quiet catches up with you whether you like it or not.

That ginger cat of mine taught me something, though. He'd sit with me, not a word between us, and it wasn't lonely. It was calm. It took me 87 years to figure out the difference.

If you're reading this, you're probably the one stuck going through my clobber. Don't bother keeping much—most of it's rubbish. But there's a photo in my wallet, one of me and my boys when they were little. Please make sure they get it. And tell them I understood why they moved away. Tell them I wasn't angry, I just missed them dreadfully. There's a big difference, you know.

Oh, and if that ginger cat's still around, give him a bit of ham for me. He was the best mate I had at the end.

Cheers, Bert Williamson

Nobody said anything for a long time.

That night, I tucked the letters into a box marked *Rainy Day Letters* and put it in my office drawer. I closed the box, Kev curled at my feet, rain still drumming on the windows. I remember thinking that if a care home could have a soul, ours was learning how to write it down.

Months later, after what happened to Kev, I'd find myself rereading Bert's letter and realising Kev had been teaching us how to say goodbye all along.

Dawn Milsom

* * *

The night shift at Rivermead is a world of its own—half dream, half domestic farce, wholly unlike the daytime rhythm. It's a time when the world slows down, and the quiet hum of the building feels almost sacred, a reminder that even in the darkest hours, life continues.

Somewhere, always, a kettle is boiling—Ruth swears the building has a ghost whose only purpose is to put kettles on and then forget about them.

"The witching hour for biscuits," Denise calls it, though she almost always works days. Ruth, who actually works nights, calls it 'the quiet chaos'—an oxymoron that somehow captures it perfectly.

Most residents sleep through, stirring only for toilet breaks. But there are always a few who don't—who can't, or won't, or whose bodies have forgotten the difference between two a.m. and two p.m. Agnes, who wanders the halls looking for her long-dead son. Harry, whose pain medication wears off around midnight. Janet, whose confusion peaks in the early hours, sending her searching for "home," a house sold years ago. Mabel, who sits by the window, gazing at her stars.

And then there's Kev who treats the night shift like his personal patrol time. He's a fixture in the shadows, a self-appointed guardian of the corridors.

One wet night, as Ruth arrived for her shift, she found Kev sitting by the staff entrance, waiting. Kev's silhouette was sharp against the dim light, his posture as deliberate as if he'd been stationed there for hours.

"Well, hello," she'd said. "Bit late for you, isn't it?" She paused, keys in hand, and raised an eyebrow. "What's the occasion, Mister?"

Kev had mrowed and walked inside like he owned the place. Which, in many ways, he did.

He proceeded to do rounds. Systematic, thorough rounds. One door at a time, pausing at each, ears swivelling to listen. If he heard steady breathing, sleep sounds, he'd move on. If he heard restlessness, confusion, distress—he'd slip inside.

Ruth had followed him that first night, fascinated. Watched him check on Agnes (sleeping peacefully, for once). Harry (awake but managing his pain). Then into Bert's room.

Bert slept like the dead—snoring that could wake the same—but Kev still checked. Sat just inside the doorway for a moment like a watchman confirming all's well, then moved on.

Dorothy was next. She kept a saucer of milk by her door "just in case," though she'd never admit to Ruth that she left it specifically for Kev. He'd lap at it delicately, leave half (good manners), then continue his patrol.

Grace. Maureen. Arthur. One by one, checking, confirming, moving on.

"He's doing rounds," Ruth reported the next morning, still amazed. "Proper rounds. Better than some staff I've worked with."

I laughed, but the truth of it lingered—a cat had become our night watchman and none of us could imagine Rivermead without him.

After that, the night team learned to read his route like a clock.

"One o'clock—he's in Grace's room," Ruth would whisper to Sasha, the Polish night care assistant. "Half one, he'll appear in the lounge. Put the kettle on."

By two, almost without fail, Kev would arrive in the office where the night team did their paperwork. Someone— usually Ruth—would open a tin of tuna "for morale".

He'd curl on the paperwork (of course), supervise log entries, occasionally bat at the computer mouse when the cursor moved across the screen. Once, he walked across the keyboard and typed a solid line of 4s across an entire care plan.

"Secret message," Sasha had declared in his thick Eastern European accent. "He's trying to tell us something."

"He's trying to tell us he wants more tuna!" Ruth replied.

But there were other nights—harder nights—when Kev's presence mattered more than anyone wanted to admit.

The night Harry's pain got too much to bear, when even the maximum medication couldn't touch it, and he lay in his bed crying with frustration and fear. Kev had appeared, climbed carefully onto the bed, and settled against Harry's side. Not purring—just there, warm and solid and real.

"Can feel his heartbeat," Harry had whispered. "Reminds me I'm still alive. Still here."

The night Agnes had a panic attack, convinced she was back in her childhood home during a fire that had killed her parents. Ruth couldn't reach her, couldn't calm her—Agnes was somewhere else entirely, somewhere terrifying.

Kev had walked in, jumped onto her lap, and pushed his head under her chin. The touch—unexpected, real, immediate—had jolted Agnes back to the present.

"Oh," she'd said, blinking. "Oh, it's the cat. I'm at Rivermead. The fire was a long time ago."

"That's right, Agnes. You're safe here."

"The cat wouldn't be here if there was a fire. Cats know these things." She'd stroked Kev's head with shaking hands. "Thank you for reminding me."

The night a new resident—William, just admitted, not adjusting well—had tried to leave at three a.m. Dressed, shoes on, walking stick in hand, determined to go "home" even though home was now a flat his family had already cleared out.

Sasha had been trying to redirect him gently when Kev appeared and simply sat in William's path. Wouldn't move. Just sat there, tail wrapped around paws, staring up at

William with those amber eyes.

"There's a cat in the way," William had said.

"There is," Sasha agreed.

"I can't just step over a cat."

"No, you can't. That would be rude."

William had considered this. "Perhaps I could sit down for a moment. Until the cat moves."

"That sounds sensible."

He'd sat. Kev had immediately jumped onto his lap. And William, stroking Kev's head, had forgotten why he needed to leave so urgently. He had then dozed off, Kev still on his lap, staying in the chair until the world made sense again and he could be ushered quietly to bed.

On quiet nights—rare but cherished—Kev when there would sit by the big window overlooking the car park. Sasha would join him sometimes, both of them watching the empty streets, the occasional car passing, the night settling over the town.

"What do you think about?" Sasha would ask him, while taking a slow drag on his cigarette.

Kev would mrow softly, as if answering.

"Me too," Sasha would say, though he had no idea what Kev had just said.

When dawn finally seeped through the blinds, Kev would follow the first footsteps of the early shift down the corridor. Pausing at every door like he was ticking names off a list. Everyone accounted for. Everyone safe. Job done.

By breakfast time, he'd be asleep on the laundry pile in the utility room, utterly spent. Staff knew to work around him, to let him rest.

"Night shift," Claire would explain to confused day staff who found a cat on the towels. "He's earned it."

One morning, I arrived early to find Ruth at the end of her shift, sitting in the office with Kev sprawled across her paperwork like a ginger paperweight.

"Rough night?"

"Not particularly. But I wanted to tell you—he's doing something remarkable, you know. These night visits. They're not just cute. They're actually therapeutic."

"I know."

"No, I mean—I've worked nights for fifteen years. Different homes, different residents. And I've never seen anything like this. He knows who needs him. Doesn't go to everyone, just the ones having difficult nights. It's like he can sense distress."

She stroked his head gently. "Last night, Janet had a nightmare. Woke up screaming. I was trying to calm her, but she was still half in the dream, not quite present. Kev appeared out of nowhere, jumped on her bed, and just sat there purring until her breathing slowed. Five minutes. That's all it took. Sasha was incredulous."

"Kev's good at his job."

"He's more than good. He's essential." Ruth looked at me seriously. "I don't know what we'll do when he's not here anymore. The night shift is going to feel very empty."

I didn't want to think about that. Not yet. But she was right—someday, Kev wouldn't be here. And the night shift, like the day shift, would have to learn how to manage without him.

But not today. Today he was here, sleeping off his patrol, secure in the knowledge that everyone was safe. That he'd done his job and done it well.

We joked that he worked nights for the overtime pay. But the truth was simpler and more profound: Kev understood that care doesn't stop when the sun goes down. That the darkness brings its own fears, its own needs. That someone —even a cat—needs to keep watch while everyone else sleeps.

I wrote in the Good Book:

Kev completed another full night shift. Ruth and Sasha

report he did his rounds, checked on everyone, intervened when Janet had a nightmare. By morning, exhausted but satisfied.

Best staff member I've ever had, and he doesn't even need coffee.

I'm grateful for every night he's here. For every round he completes. For every life he touches in the darkness.

The truth was, the home would feel emptier without his soft-footed patrols.

***

Early October brought more rain and a surprise CQC inspection.

I got the call at nine in the morning: they'd be there by eleven. My stomach dropped. We were doing well—I knew we were doing well—but inspections always found something to be nitpicky on as if to prove they were doing their job. Some minor infraction, some paperwork not quite right, some process that needed tightening.

"Right," I told the staff in a hasty meeting. "Everyone knows what to do. Documentation up to date, building clean, residents happy. We've got this."

We did not, in fact, have this.

The inspector, Amanda Harper, was a woman in her mid-fifties, her sharp features framed by severe 1950s style glasses and a demeanour that hinted she'd witnessed it all—and found little of it worth her time. She arrived armed with a clipboard and trailed by a junior inspector who wore the unmistakable air of someone who'd rather be anywhere but here.

With her clipboard held firmly in her pale hands, Amanda strode down the corridors, the sharp click of her heels echoing off the walls. Her assistant trailed behind, his expression still unmistakably wishing he were elsewhere.

The first hour went fine. Documentation was in order. Building was clean. Residents were, generally speaking, happy.

Then we got to risk assessments.

"I see you have a therapy animal program," Caroline remarked, her tone clipped as she leafed through the files. She paused, adjusting the frames of her glasses with a deliberate push, as though double-checking the name she'd just read. "A cat named..." She hesitated, her brow furrowing slightly. "Kev."

"That's right."

"And this is a stray cat? Who comes and goes as he pleases?"

"Well, yes, but he's fully vaccinated, health-checked, and we have comprehensive documentation—"

"I'd like to see that documentation."

I pulled out the Kev file, which had grown substantially over the summer. Vet records, vaccination certificates, risk assessments, incident reports (all zero incidents), staff training on animal handling, consent forms from residents' families, testimonials from the residents themselves.

Caroline read through it all in silence. Then: "This is highly irregular."

"It is," I admitted. "But it's also been remarkably beneficial for our residents. We've seen improvements in mood, reduction in anxiety, better engagement with activities—"

"That's all very nice, but there are protocols. This cat could pose infection risks, allergy issues, injury from scratching or biting."

"We've had no incidents in ten months."

"Yet." She made a note. "I'll need to observe this animal's next visit. When does he come?"

I checked my watch. "Actually, he should be here any minute."

Amanda looked like she'd swallowed something sour. "Perfect. I'll observe."

Right on cue, there was a mrow from the French windows. Kev had arrived.

I let him in, and he paused in the doorway, taking in the scene: me, looking stressed; Amanda, looking stern; the junior inspector, looking bored; and various residents looking hopeful.

Kev made a decision.

He walked directly to Amanda Harper and began weaving between her legs.

"Nnn—," Amanda said, trying to step away.

Kev persisted.

"I said—would you stop that?"

Kev sat down at her feet and stared up at her with his most winning expression.

I held my breath. This could go very badly.

Amanda looked down at Kev. Kev looked up at Amanda. Something passed between them—some wordless communication that I wasn't privy to.

"Fine," Amanda said. "But I'm watching you."

She sat down in one of the lounge chairs, and Kev immediately jumped into her lap.

"No. Absolutely not. I'm here in a professional capacity—"

Kev began purring.

Amanda's hand, as if operating independently from her brain, began to stroke Kev's head. "I'm still observing," she said, but her voice had lost some of its edge.

Over the next hour, I watched Amanda Harper's transformation. She sat with Kev on her lap while residents came to chat. She heard Dorothy talk about how Kev had helped her feel less lonely after her sister died. She watched Arthur do his physio exercises with Kev supervising, noting how much more motivated he seemed. She even witnessed the tail end of Grace's reading session, Grace stumbling through Dickens while Kev listened attentively.

But the clincher was Janet.

Janet had been having a bad day. She'd woken up confused and agitated, asking for people long dead, convinced she needed to be somewhere she couldn't name. Nothing we did had helped, and Tom had phoned to say he couldn't visit today—a work emergency—which had made everything even worse.

Kev, still on Amanda's lap, suddenly looked up. His ears swivelled toward the conservatory where Janet was pacing, wringing her hands, that dementia anxiety rising.

Before anyone could stop him, Kev jumped down and trotted over to Janet.

"Mrow," he said definitively.

Janet stopped pacing. "Kev?"

He rubbed against her legs, and Amanda watched as Janet's whole body seemed to soften. Her hands unclenched. Her breathing slowed.

"It's afternoon," Janet said, clearer than she'd been all day. "You come in the afternoons."

Kev mrowed his agreement.

"Can you sit with me?"

He could, and he did, and within minutes Janet was calm, stroking his fur, telling him about a ginger cat from her childhood—whether true or confabulated didn't matter. She was present. She was okay.

Amanda watched all this in silence. When she finally spoke, her voice was different—softer, thoughtful.

"How long has this been going on?"

"Since March. Five months."

"And you've seen consistent benefits?"

"We have. Not just mood and anxiety—though those have definitely improved. But physical benefits too. Arthur's arthritis is easier when he's stroking Kev. Grace's speech therapy has accelerated. Even our staff—" I thought of Alicia, of that day in the staff room. And Zainab, the student doctor. "They've benefitted."

Amanda made notes. Then she looked at me directly. "This is still highly irregular."

My heart sank.

"However," she continued, "it's also clearly effective. And your documentation is exemplary." She glanced back at Janet, at the peace on her face. "I'm going to recommend this as a best practice case study. With your permission, I'd like our training department to contact you about developing guidelines based on your programme."

I stared at her. "Really?"

"Really." She almost smiled. Almost. "That cat is doing more for these residents than some qualified therapists I've seen. It would be remiss of me not to acknowledge that."

The junior inspector, who'd been silent this whole time, piped up: "Can I pet the cat?"

"No," Amanda said. "We're still on duty. But..." She looked at Kev, who was still with Janet. "He is rather exceptional, isn't he?"

"He is," I agreed.

We passed the inspection. Not just passed—we got an Outstanding rating, the first in Rivermead's history. I sat in my office afterwards, staring at the certificate on the wall, and felt a strange mix of pride and sadness. Kev had done this. Not me, not the staff, but a scruffy ginger cat who'd wandered in off the street. I wondered if he knew how much he'd changed us.

I wondered if he cared. And then I laughed—of course he knew. Of course he cared. That's who he was.

That night, the staff went to the pub—all of us who could, even Sasha who normally went straight home after shifts. We raised our pints to Kev, to Outstanding ratings, to somehow surviving the impossible.

"None of this happens without him," Denise said, slightly drunk and very emotional. "The cat did this. The actual literal cat."

"The cat helped," I corrected. "We did it too. We chose to say yes when he showed up. We chose to make it work."

"Still the cat," Denise insisted. "Don't diminish his contribution. He's staff. Best staff. Staff of the year."

We all drank to that, and someone—probably Claire—took a photo of us all holding up our phones with pictures of Kev on the screens.

It's still in the staff room, that photo. Fifteen people, slightly drunk, holding up glowing screens showing the same orange cat from fifteen different angles.

Under it, someone wrote: "The team that a cat built."

And you know what? That's exactly what we were.

CQC inspection. Amanda Harper, one of their toughest inspectors, was won over by Kev within minutes. He spent the afternoon demonstrating, without any coaching from us, exactly why this programme matters. The inspector called him "exceptional." She's right. He is.

But that wasn't the whole truth, and I knew it. Kev wasn't just exceptional. He was essential. Somewhere along the way, this scruffy stray had become the beating heart of Rivermead, and I couldn't imagine how we'd ever functioned without him.

***

Kev, now 10 months into his reign, strutted through the home like he owned it. The residents adored him—Maureen knitted him a tiny scarf, which he tolerated for exactly ten seconds before shaking it off with a look of mild disdain. But Kev, with his uncanny psychic intuition, knew something was amiss that morning. He had lingered outside Dorothy's door longer than usual, his amber eyes fixed on the wood as if sensing the stillness within.

It was Claire who found Dorothy a few moments later. She'd gone to wake her for breakfast—Dorothy was usually an early riser, but her curtains were still drawn at eight o'clock. Claire had knocked, waited, knocked again. Then opened the door.

Dorothy was in bed, lying on her side, one hand resting on the patchwork quilt that Kev liked to sleep on when he visited. She looked peaceful. More than peaceful—she looked like someone who'd simply decided to stop, gently and without any fuss.

Claire checked for a pulse anyway. Protocol. But she already knew.

"Dawn?" Her voice over the phone was steady but tight. "Can you come to Dorothy's room? It's... she's gone."

I was there in two minutes. Found Claire sitting in Dorothy's chair by the window, staring at nothing.

"Natural causes," she said. "In her sleep. The way everyone hopes to go."

"Have you called—"

"Doc is on his way. I just... I needed a minute before we start all the procedures."

I sat down beside her.

"She was fine yesterday," Claire said. "Ate all her lunch. Did the crossword. Told me about a poem she was working on. And then..." She gestured helplessly.

"That's how it goes sometimes."

"I hate it. I hate that we don't get to prepare. Don't get to say goodbye properly."

"She said goodbye," I reminded her gently. "Last week, remember? When she gave you that poem she wrote about nursing. She said 'keep this safe for me.' That was goodbye."

Claire's face crumpled slightly, but she held it together. "I suppose it was."

The rest of the morning was a blur of procedures. Doctor's visit, death certificate, funeral home, family arriving. Dorothy's son and daughter-in-law coming, red-eyed but composed. They'd been expecting this—Dorothy was ninety-one, had been declining slowly—but expectation doesn't make loss easier.

"She loved it here," her son said, looking around the room at the photos, the books, the carefully organised life. "She was happier these last two years than she'd been since Dad died. Said she'd found her tribe."

"She was part of ours too," I said.

What I didn't tell him, what I couldn't quite articulate, was how much Dorothy had mattered. Not just as a resident, but as a presence. She'd created a photo album of Kev. Had written poems about the residents, about the staff, about life in a place where people came to die but somehow still managed to live.

By afternoon, the room had been cleared. Family had taken what they wanted—photos, jewellery, the poetry notebooks. The rest would be donated or disposed of. Within hours, Dorothy's room looked like she'd never been there at all.

That's what disturbed the residents most, I think. Not the death itself—they were used to people dying—but the speed of erasure. How quickly someone's entire life could be packed into boxes and removed.

"She was here yesterday," Maureen said, staring at the empty room. "How can she just be... gone?"

The afternoon felt wrong. Too quiet. Too normal. Lunch happened, activities happened, medication rounds happened. The machinery of care rolled on because it had to, because the living still needed caring for.

But Dorothy's chair in the lounge stayed empty. Nobody sat in it.

Kev came back at two o'clock—his usual time—and went straight to Dorothy's door. It was closed now, would stay closed until we had a new resident.

He sat outside it for a long time. Not meowing, not scratching. Just sitting, tail wrapped around his paws, staring at the closed door like he was waiting for it to open.

"Kev?" I approached carefully. "She's not there, love. She's gone."

He looked at me once, then back at the door. Waiting.

"Come on. Let's go see the others."

He refused to move.

I left him there, went to do my rounds. When I came back half an hour later, he was still there. Still waiting.

"He knows," Bert said. He'd been watching from his doorway. "Don't ask me how, but he knows. He knew this morning before any of us did."

Finally, around three o'clock, Kev stood. He looked at the door one more time, then walked into the lounge and jumped onto Dorothy's chair.

The residents held their breath.

He circled once, twice, three times—the way cats do when they're settling. Then he sat down, very deliberately, in the exact centre of the seat. Not lying down, not relaxing. Just sitting, upright and alert, like he was keeping vigil.

"He's waiting for her," Grace said softly.

"He's saying goodbye," Maureen corrected.

We left him there. Through the rest of the afternoon, through dinner, through the evening. Staff worked around him. Residents came and went, but nobody tried to move him, nobody suggested he go elsewhere.

He just sat in Dorothy's chair, keeping watch.

At nine o'clock, Ruth came on for night shift. "He's still there?"

"Still there."

"Should we... I don't know. Do something?"

"Let him be. He's processing."

"He's a cat."

"He's Kev. Different rules."

Around midnight, Ruth texted me. I was home by then, trying to sleep, failing.

"He moved," she said.

I called her back. "Where?"

"Into Dorothy's room. The door was closed, but he... I don't know how, but he got in. Sasha found him sitting on her bed, on that quilt she had. Just sitting there in the dark."

"Leave him. If he needs to be there, let him be there."

"Dawn, it's a bit creepy. A cat sitting in a dead woman's room in the middle of the night."

"It's Kev doing what Kev does. Saying goodbye in his own way."

She was quiet for a moment. "Alright. But I'm leaving the door open. I'm not having him trapped in there all night."

When I arrived for the early shift the next morning, Kev was gone. Ruth said he'd left around five, walking slowly, tail low. Not his usual confident stride—something more subdued, more final.

"He went to every resident's room," Ruth told me. "Like he was checking on everyone. Making sure they were okay. Then he went to the French windows and waited to be let out. Didn't even want breakfast."

The residents felt Dorothy's absence differently. Some were matter-of-fact about it—people died, that's what happened in care homes, you got used to it. Others were quietly devastated.

But it was Maureen who articulated what we were all feeling.

"It's not just that she's gone," she said. "It's that Kev's sad. And if Kev's sad, it makes it more real somehow. Like her death mattered enough to make even a cat grieve."

Grace, struggling for words as always, managed: "He... he loved her. In his... cat way. Loved her."

The next time Kev visited, he went straight to Dorothy's chair again. But this time he didn't sit in vigil. He jumped up, circled once, then jumped down and walked away.

The message was clear: she's really gone. The goodbye is

Kev, the Care Home Cat

over. Life continues.

He never sat in that chair again. Not once in all the weeks that followed. Even when other residents tried to encourage him, offered treats, patted the cushion invitingly—he'd refuse. As if that chair belonged to Dorothy's memory and he wouldn't disrespect it by claiming it as his own.

We held a memorial service that week. Small, simple. Dorothy's family came. Residents gathered. I read one of her poems—one about Kev.

Love Dressed in Fur

Soft paws tread with a velvet grace,
A ginger glow, a sunlit face.
Whiskers twitch, a curious stare,
Love incarnate, beyond compare.

Your purr, a hymn, so warm, so near,
A symphony only my heart can hear.
In amber eyes, the world feels right,
A flicker of flame in the quiet night.

Your fur, a hearth where comfort lies,
A golden glow beneath the skies.
In every leap, in every sprawl,
You're love itself, my ginger call.
So here you stay, my heart's true muse,
In every purr, I'm yours to choose.
Love dressed in fur, my fiery friend,
A bond unbroken, without end."

By the time I finished, there wasn't a dry eye in the room.

Afterwards, Bert came to find me. "She'd have liked that. The service. Simple, no fuss. Dorothy was never one for fuss."

"She wasn't."

"But she mattered. I want you to know that. She documented things, remembered things. Made sure we weren't forgotten." He paused, uncomfortable with emotion as always. "When I die, there won't be much record I was here. No poems, no photos, no archive. But Dorothy wrote about me once. In one of her poems. So maybe there will be something. Maybe that's enough."

I thought about the notebooks Dorothy had left—full of poems about residents, staff, daily life at Rivermead. Her family had donated them to us, said Dorothy would have wanted them to stay where they were written.

That night, going through Dorothy's poems, I found one I hadn't seen before. Dated three days before she died.

Whispers to the Ginger Cat

When I leave this place,
Tell the ginger cat not to mope.
I'll visit in the sunlight if I can,
A warm breeze through the window,
A golden glow on the sill.
Look for me in the flicker of dust motes,
In the patch of sun where you nap.
I'll be the soft rustle of leaves,
The quiet hum of a lazy afternoon.
Do not grieve, my faithful friend,
For love lingers in the light.
When the sun spills across your fur,
Know it's me, holding you tight.

I copied it to the Good Book, along with my own entry:

Dorothy died peacefully in her sleep last week. Kev mourned her. Sat vigil in her chair all afternoon, spent the night in her empty room. The next day he checked on every resident, making sure everyone else was okay, then left. When he came back the next time, he said goodbye to her chair one final time, then moved on.

The residents say if Kev grieves, it makes the death more real. They're right. His sadness gave them permission for their own. His goodbye showed them how to let go.

Dorothy's last poem said to tell the cat not to mope. She promised to visit in the sunlight if she could. Today, bright autumn sun came through the French Doors. Kev sat in the beam for an hour, eyes closed, purring. I'd like to think she kept her promise.

Goodbye, Dorothy.

And on sunny days, when light streamed through the lounge windows, Kev would sit in the beams and purr.

Dorothy, keeping her promise. Visiting in the sunlight when she could.

Maybe it was true. Maybe it wasn't. But it comforted us to believe it. And comfort, in a place like Rivermead, was worth more than proof.

***

It was nearly eleven when the call came from the night team.

I was at Adam's flat—a rare evening off, halfway through a Netflix series neither of us was really watching, his arm around my shoulders, both of us drowsy and content. My phone buzzed on the coffee table. Ruth's name on the screen.

I answered immediately, that familiar spike of adrenaline cutting through the drowsiness. "What's wrong?"

"Dawn, sorry to call. It's not an emergency—well, not quite. But Mr. Phillips is having breathing difficulties. Respiratory rate elevated, O2 sats dropping. I've called the on-call GP, but she's an hour away and I think we need someone here now. He's getting anxious, which is making it worse."

Denis Phillips. Eighty-four, COPD, prone to panic when he couldn't catch his breath—which of course made the breathing worse, a vicious cycle.

"I'm coming. Give him the oxygen, sit him upright, stay calm. I'll be there in twenty minutes."

I was already reaching for my shoes before I hung up.

"Everything okay?" Adam asked, though he was already standing too, picking up my bag, his keys.

"Resident with breathing problems. I need to—"

"I'll drive you."

"Adam, you don't have to—"

"I know I don't have to. But you've had wine, I haven't, and I'd rather you got there in one piece. Come on."

We made it in fifteen minutes, Adam driving with the calm efficiency of someone who'd dealt with his own share of emergencies in schools. He didn't ask questions, didn't complain about the interrupted evening, just drove while I mentally ran through protocols.

When we arrived, I turned to him. "This might take a while. You should go home—"

"I'll wait. Unless you'd rather I didn't?"

I looked at him properly. Saw genuine concern, no resentment. No martyred patience or pointed sighs.

"You can come in if you want. There's a staff room. Might be boring."

"I brought my book. I'm good at boring."

Denis was in his room, Ruth beside him, oxygen mask on, clearly fighting for each breath. His eyes were wide with fear—that terrible primal panic of not being able to breathe.

"Mr. Phillips, I'm here. You're alright. We've got you." I checked his stats—oxygen low but not dangerously so, respiratory rate too fast. Mostly panic. "I need you to breathe with me. Slow. In through your nose, out through your mouth. With me now."

I demonstrated, exaggerating the movements. Ruth joined in. Slowly, painfully slowly, Denis's breathing began to match ours. The panic in his eyes receded slightly.

We stayed like that for twenty minutes. Breathing together. Ruth monitoring stats. Me talking him through it, keeping my voice low and calm even though my heart was racing.

"That's it. You're doing so well. The oxygen's helping. Your levels are coming back up. Just keep breathing with me."

When the GP finally arrived, Mr. Phillips was stable. Still on oxygen, still being monitored, but out of immediate danger.

"Probably an infection brewing," the GP said after examining him. "I'll prescribe antibiotics. Keep him on oxygen overnight. If he deteriorates, call 999, but I think he'll be fine."

After the GP had left, after we'd settled Denis for the night with medication and reassurance, I found Adam in the staff room exactly where I'd left him. Book open, mug of tea beside him. He looked up when I came in.

"How is he?"

"Stable. Scared himself more than anything, but he'll be okay." I collapsed onto the sofa beside him. "I'm sorry. This is not how I planned our evening."

"It's fine."

"It's not fine. We had plans. A nice evening. And instead you're sitting in a care home staff room at midnight."

"Dawn." He closed his book, turned to face me properly. "This is your life. This is what you do. If I couldn't handle interrupted evenings and emergency calls, I'd have walked away months ago."

"Most people would have."

"I'm not most people."

I felt something tight in my chest loosen slightly. "Thank

you for driving me. For staying."

"Of course. Though I should probably thank whoever made me tea. That was above and beyond."

We sat in comfortable silence for a moment. Then Adam said, "Can I ask you something?"

"Sure."

"Do you ever get used to it? The fear? The responsibility? Knowing that someone's life might depend on you making the right call?"

I thought about it. "Not really. You get better at managing it, staying calm under pressure. But the fear never completely goes away. Which is probably good—means you still care, still take it seriously."

"How often does this happen? Emergency calls in the middle of the night?"

"Often enough. Maybe once a month, something that needs me specifically. More if you count calls just to update me or ask advice." I looked at him. "Is that going to be a problem? Because I can't change it. This is the job."

"I know. And no, it's not a problem. I just want to understand. Want to know what your life actually looks like, not some idealised version." He paused. "My teaching—it's stressful, but it's contained. School hours, marking in the evening, but my weekends are mostly mine. Your work bleeds into everything. I'm realising that."

"It does. I'm sorry."

"Stop apologising. I'm not complaining—just observing."

Ruth appeared in the doorway. "Mr. Phillips is asking for you. Just wants to say goodnight properly."

I went. Found Denis drowsy from medication but calmer, oxygen still on but breathing easier.

"Thank you, Dawn," he whispered. "Sorry for the bother."

"Never a bother. That's what I'm here for. You rest now."

When I came back, Adam was making fresh tea for the

night staff—apparently he'd been recruited.

"Ruth says you're a keeper. And I make tea wrong, but she's willing to overlook it given my obvious other qualities."

"Which are?"

"She didn't specify. I'm assuming my stunning good looks and charming personality."

"Obviously. I suspect Denise has mentioned the cake you normally arrive armed with though." I winked.

It was after midnight when we finally sat down. The home had that odd stillness it gets at night—humming lights, the distant tick of the fish tank filter.

Kev appeared from nowhere, tail flicking, his coat shining in the dim glow. He jumped onto the sofa between us, a warm, purring barrier.

Adam smiled. "He's doing his rounds, isn't he?"

"Always." I grinned as I got a head bonk.

We stayed another hour—Adam somehow getting drawn into a debate with Ruth about whether *The Great British Bake Off* had declined since moving to Channel 4.

By the time we left, it was past one. The drive home was quiet, both of us tired.

"Thank you," I said as we pulled up outside my flat. "Really. For tonight. For understanding."

"Thank you for letting me see this side of your work. For trusting me with it." He kissed me gently. "Get some sleep. Text me when you wake up."

"I love you."

"I love you too. Even though you make tea wrong."

"Ruth said you—"

"I know what Ruth said. I'm deflecting. Go to bed."

I went inside, exhausted but somehow lighter than before. Because he'd been there. He'd seen the reality—the interrupted evening, the stress, the way work bled into everything—and he hadn't run. Hadn't complained. Had just been there, calm and present and useful.

I wrote in the Good Book before sleeping:

Late-night call for Denis—breathing difficulties, panic, eventually stabilised. Standard emergency. Adam was there. Saw the reality of the job, not the sanitised version. Drove me, waited, made tea for the night staff, stayed until past one a.m.

He didn't complain. Didn't make me feel guilty for the interrupted evening. Just adapted. Just helped. Just was.

Kev was right about him. Of course Kev was right.

The next morning, I found a text from Adam sent at two-thirty a.m.:

Made it home. Ruth's right about the tea thing—I googled proper technique. Will practice. You're amazing at your job. Don't forget that. Sleep well. x

I saved that message. Kept it for the hard days, the days when I questioned whether I was good enough, doing enough, being enough.

Because sometimes love looks like midnight drives and terrible tea and hours in staff rooms. Sometimes it looks like someone seeing your whole complicated life and saying: yes, I'll have that. All of it. Even the interrupted evenings. Especially those.

* * *

September brought a request I wasn't expecting.

Tom came to my office on a Tuesday afternoon, looking nervous. He'd been visiting Janet almost daily for the months she'd been with us, and I'd watched him age in that time—the particular ageing that comes from grief without resolution.

"I wanted to ask you something," he said. "It might be strange."

"Try me."

"Janet and I... we got married forty-three years ago. On September 22nd, actually." He paused, gathering himself.

"Our anniversary is in a couple of weeks, and I thought... I know she doesn't always remember me. I know she doesn't remember the wedding. But I thought maybe we could do something small. Here. To mark it. Is that ridiculous?"

"It's not ridiculous at all."

"Just something simple. Me, Janet, maybe cake. Nothing elaborate. I don't want to upset her or confuse her. But I can't let it pass without..." His voice broke. "Without doing something."

I thought about this. About the cruelty of dementia, how it steals not just memories but futures, the milestones you thought you'd have together. About Tom, who showed up every single day to visit a wife who often didn't know who he was, and how he deserved something beautiful.

"What if we did afternoon tea?" I suggested. "In the garden, if the weather holds. You, Janet, a few of the other residents who she's friendly with. Nice cake."

"Did someone say cake?" Denise popped her head around the door, flashing a thumbs up before turning back to help Florence make her way to the loo.

"Could Kev come?" asked Tom.

The question surprised me, though it shouldn't have. Kev had become part of Janet's life, a constant in a world of confusion.

"I'm sure he'd be delighted to attend if he doesn't have any other cat commitments in his diary."

We planned it carefully. Not a vow renewal—too complicated, too likely to confuse Janet. Just a special afternoon tea, a celebration of marriage and endurance and love that persisted even when memory didn't.

September 22nd dawned sunny and warm, the kind of perfect Indian summer day that felt like a gift. We set up tables in the garden, draping them with white lacy cloths and arranging the pretty blue and white china Adam and I had found at a car boot sale the previous Sunday.

Margaret had brought flowers from her daughter's garden, adding a splash of colour and charm. Denise, of course, had baked the cake—not a wedding cake, just a simple sponge, but she'd poured extra care into it. Her artistic flair shone through in the delicate sugar icing bride and groom figures she'd crafted.

Tom arrived at two, wearing his best suit. He'd brought photographs, old ones from their wedding, young Tom and young Janet smiling at a camera in 1980, their whole lives ahead of them. It was beautiful and tragic all at the same time.

Janet was having a medium day—not her best, not her worst. She knew Tom was someone important, even if she couldn't always access why.

"You look smart," she said when she saw him.

"It's a special day."

"Is it?"

"It is. It's our anniversary. Forty-three years married."

Janet frowned, reaching for a memory that wouldn't come. "Married?"

I saw Tom's face crumble just slightly before he recovered. "To me. You married me. Best day of my life."

"Oh." She considered this. "Was it a nice wedding?"

"Beautiful." He showed her the photographs, and she studied them with interest, not recognition—just looking at two strangers who happened to be very happy.

"They look nice," she said.

"That's us," Tom said gently. "That's you and me."

"Oh," she said again, and I saw the flash of distress that came when the world stopped making sense. "I don't... I can't..."

That's when Kev arrived.

He'd been making his usual rounds indoors—nimbly evading Denise's attempts to fasten a tiny dickie bow around his neck—and somehow, he seemed to sense he was needed.

Without hesitation, he headed straight for Janet and leapt gracefully into her lap.

"Kev!" She brightened immediately, the distress fading. "It must be two o'clock!"

"It is," Tom said, grateful for the intervention. "And Kev came to help us celebrate."

The afternoon proceeded in a strange but lovely way. We had tea and cake. Arthur made a slightly ribald toast that made everyone laugh. Maureen told a story about her own wedding.

And Janet, with Kev on her lap, seemed content. She didn't remember the wedding or even really understand what they were celebrating, but she understood that people she cared about were gathered, that there was cake, that Tom kept holding her hand with fierce tenderness.

"This is nice," she said more than once. "This is very nice."

The best moment came toward the end. Tom had brought their wedding song—"The First Time Ever I Saw Your Face," by Roberta Flack—and he asked if he could play it.

As the music started, something shifted in Janet's face. Not full recognition, but something. A sense-memory perhaps, body remembering what mind couldn't.

"I know this," she said slowly.

"It's our song," Tom told her. "We danced to it at our wedding."

"Did we?"

"We did. Would you like to dance now?"

She looked uncertain, but Tom was already standing, offering his hand. And Janet, with the particular bravery required to step into the unknown, took it.

They swayed together in the garden, not really dancing, just holding each other while the music played. Janet had her head on Tom's shoulder, and Tom had his eyes closed, and I saw tears tracking down his face.

Kev watched from his chair, tail swishing slightly, those amber eyes taking in the scene with what I could only describe as approval.

When the song ended, Janet pulled back and looked at Tom. For a moment—just a moment—I saw recognition flash across her face. Not just *this is someone important* but *this is Tom, my Tom.*

"I love you," she said, clear as a bell.

Tom's breath caught. "I love you too. So much."

"Even though I'm..." She gestured vaguely at her own head, trying to encompass all that had been lost.

"Especially now," Tom said. "Always."

The moment passed, and Janet looked confused again, not quite sure where she was or why this man was crying. But it had been real. I'd seen it. We'd all seen it.

After Janet had been taken inside for her afternoon nap, Tom lingered in the garden. I sat with him while he composed himself, while he processed what had just happened.

"Thank you," he said finally. "For today. For all of this. For Kev."

"Kev just showed up. He's his own cat."

"But you let him stay. You made this possible." He looked at me directly. "You have no idea what this means. To have one last good memory. One moment when she knew me. I'll carry that with me after... after."

We both knew what after meant. After Janet was gone. After this long goodbye finally ended.

"I'm glad we could do this for you," I said quietly.

That night, I added to the Good Book:

September 22nd: Tom and Janet's 43rd wedding anniversary. Celebrated with (amazing) afternoon tea, cake, and dancing. Janet had a moment of clarity, of real recognition. Tom will remember this. I'll remember this. Kev

bore witness to enduring love, the kind that doesn't quit even when everything else does. He seems to understand that some occasions require his presence. Or maybe he just likes cake.
Either way, I'm grateful he was here.

I later attached one of the photos—Tom and Janet dancing, Kev visible in the background, the garden golden with late afternoon light. Evidence of beauty in a place people associate with endings.

Proof that even here, even now, there was still life to be lived.

A week after the anniversary party, Tom stopped by my office .

"I had that hour. That perfect hour. That's more than most people get at the end. That's... that's everything, really."

He stood to leave, then paused at the door. "When Kev dies—and I know he will, eventually—you make sure everyone knows what he did. Not just the big things. The small things. The one-hour miracles. Those matter most."

"I will," I promised.

This book is that promise kept.

***

Late October had transformed the oak tree at the centre of the garden, its leaves now a rich tapestry of bronze and gold. With every gust of wind, the leaves broke free, spiralling across the lawn like delicate, fleeting memories carried on the breeze.

The light slanted low and golden, beautiful yet tinged with melancholy, a quiet reminder that the year was winding down and darker days lay ahead.

And by October, Adam had finally found his rhythm at Rivermead. He'd started volunteering on Saturday mornings, though "volunteering" often meant playing a supporting role in the lives of its colourful residents. There were the activities, of course—bingo, knitting circles, the occasional sing-along (the Kev Choir was still going strong) —but more often than not, "helping" meant 'being talked at by Bert about the failings of modern Britain' or patiently holding skeins of wool while Agnes wound them into balls.

The residents loved him. More importantly, they'd accepted him—not as a visitor, but as part of the fabric of the place.

"Your Adam fixed the blind in my room," Maureen told me one afternoon. "Didn't make a fuss, just did it."

"He's teaching me to read better," Grace added, her speech clearer these days. "Slowly. With patience."

Even Janet seemed to recognise him, would smile when he appeared, though she still couldn't hold onto who he was from visit to visit.

But it was Kev's opinion that mattered most to the residents.

One Saturday, I found Adam in the lounge with Kev sprawled across his lap, both of them reading—Adam a novel, Kev presumably contemplating the mysteries of the universe.

Arthur was watching from his chair. "Cat's made his decision about you, then."

"Seems like it," Adam agreed.

"Good. Kev's never wrong about people." Arthur tapped his newspaper sagely.

Later, helping clear lunch dishes, Adam asked, "Do they know it's serious? You and me?"

I nearly dropped a plate. "Is it? Serious?"

He stopped, looked at me properly. "I'm spending my Saturdays at a care home, Dawn. I'm learning the names of twenty elderly people and their various medication schedules. I bought special treats for a therapy cat. Yes, it's serious."

"Oh."

"Is that okay?"

I thought about it. About how seamlessly he'd slipped into this strange life of mine. About how he never complained when I cancelled plans, just rescheduled. About how he'd learned to read my tiredness levels and know when I needed company versus solitude.

"Yes," I said. "It's very okay."

He kissed me over a stack of teacups, and somewhere behind us, Denise made approving noises that we both ignored.

That afternoon, I updated the Good Book:

Adam's become part of the furniture. Residents approve. Kev approves. I more than approve. Strange to think six months ago I was convinced I was too busy for love. Maybe I wasn't too busy. Maybe I was just waiting for someone who understood that care work isn't competition—it's context.

Also: Kev definitely orchestrated this entire relationship. Taking full credit, the smug bastard.

Kev appeared, leaping gracefully onto the windowsill to stretch with feline ease. He looked weary today—not sick, not yet, but slower, his movements more deliberate. I sat quietly, watching the rhythmic flick of his tail, catching the sunlight, perfectly in tune with the gentle twitches of his nose as he slipped into a dream. Dust motes floated lazily around him, suspended in the golden haze of the afternoon.

I thought again of Dorothy and her words.

You never realise you're living the good old days until they're gone. It's only in hindsight that they earn their name, after they've slipped through your fingers, and the present is so easily overlooked. That quiet moment with Kev—his peaceful presence, the sunlight illuminating his ginger fur like a halo—is a memory I'll hold close forever. Because it was the moment just before everything changed.

***

It started so quietly none of us could have said when exactly it began.

Looking back, there were signs. Small things. Kev sleeping more during visits. Taking longer to get up after naps. Choosing the sunny spots on the floor rather than jumping onto laps. But cats sleep. Cats prefer warm spots. Nothing seemed obviously wrong.

It was Mrs. Patterson who first said something. "Have you noticed he's not quite himself?" she said, catching me in the corridor. "A little quieter than usual."

"Probably just the weather," I said, wanting to believe it. "Everyone's sluggish when it turns damp."

"Maybe," Mrs. P said, but she didn't sound convinced.

We all agreed it was probably nothing. Just age. Just autumn. Just one of those things.

It was easier that way.

But over the following weeks, the changes became harder to ignore.

Kev still came for his visits, still did his rounds. But the rounds got shorter. He'd greet Maureen, spend time with Bert, check on Grace—but then he'd find a sunny spot and sleep for the rest of the afternoon. No more full tours of the building. No more checking every room. Just the essentials, then rest.

"He's earned it," Denise said when I mentioned it. "Eight years old—that's middle-aged for a cat. Let him take it easier."

The residents started adapting without discussion. If Kev was sleeping in the window, they'd move their chairs closer to him rather than expecting him to come to them. If he didn't feel like jumping onto laps, they'd sit beside him. Small accommodations, barely acknowledged, but collectively significant.

Grace left her blanket folded neatly on his favourite chair "so he won't get cold."

Bert started slipping him bits of ham every visit, muttering, "Got to keep his strength up, lad."

Even Arthur, who'd once claimed to merely tolerate cats, started saving corners of his crossword for Kev to sit on—not because Kev wanted to read the puzzle, but because Arthur wanted him nearby.

"He's getting on," Arthur said when I asked about it. "When you're getting on, you need people to make allowances. Simple as that."

One day in early November, Kev arrived for his visit and immediately went to sleep in the sunny patch by the French windows. Didn't greet anyone. Didn't do rounds. Just walked to the sun, circled once, and collapsed into sleep.

The residents exchanged worried glances but said nothing. Just rearranged their afternoon around him—chairs pulled close, voices kept low, everyone orienting toward the sleeping cat like he was the sun they orbited.

After two hours, he woke, stretched, did a cursory round of his closest friends, then went to the door to leave. The whole visit had been subdued, minimal, nothing like his usual engaged presence.

"He's not himself," Maureen said after he'd gone.

"He's not a young cat any more," I replied, though the words felt wrong even as I said them.

That evening, I called Mrs Patterson. "Hopefully it's nothing. But we should take him to the vet. I can pay—"

Mrs P agreed to take Kev in the following morning.

After we hung up, I sat in my office for a long time, staring at nothing. Because I knew. Somewhere deep down, where instinct lives, I knew this wasn't just age or weather or tiredness.

Something was wrong with Kev.

Still, it was hard to worry when he'd seemed so content. He'd sit in the window light for hours, tail tucked neatly, eyes half-closed. The residents would talk around him like parishioners around a saint.

That afternoon Bert had said, "He's listening differently. Like he already knows the end of the story."

"Don't be morbid," I told him, and everyone laughed, including Kev, who chose that moment to yawn and stretch.

But later that evening, as I locked up my office, I caught sight of him in the hallway — not asleep, just sitting, staring at nothing, utterly still.

Something in the air shifted, thin as a thread. I've learned to trust my instincts about residents. When someone's about to take a turn, there's a quality to the air around them—something I can't name but always recognise. A thinness, maybe. A sense that they're already partly elsewhere, one foot in this world and one foot out.

I felt it around Kev that November afternoon. That same thinness. That same sense of something ending, whether we were ready or not. I told myself I was being paranoid. Projecting. Catastrophising because I'd been doing this job too long and seen too many deaths. Scared because I loved Kev too much.

But deep down, I knew. The way you know things before your conscious mind will admit them.

Kev was saying goodbye. Not today, not tomorrow, but soon.

And there was nothing I could do but witness it. Be present for it. Love him through it, the way he'd taught us to love everyone through everything.

The building around me was utterly silent now, shrouded by the deepening darkness. Stepping outside, the chill of the November air bit at my skin as I made my way to my car. Above me, the sky stretched vast and clear, the stars piercing through the cold with their unwavering light. Mabel's stars —those steadfast companions that remained unchanged even as the world crumbled around them.

My thoughts turned to Kev, and a quiet ache settled in

my chest.

"Hang on," I murmured, my breath visible in the frosty air. The words were meant for the stars, for the universe, for whatever might be listening. "Just a little longer. Let us say goodbye the way we should. Let us have that, at least."

***

The morning Mrs Patterson took him in, the sky was the colour of tin — flat, metallic, unforgiving. The kind of morning that pressed on your shoulders like a weight you couldn't shrug off.

Kev sat by the front door, his tail curled neatly around his paws, as if he'd somehow understood the day's plan and chosen not to resist. Normally, the mere clatter of his carrier would send him darting for cover—under the couch, behind the radiator, anywhere out of sight. But today, he stepped inside without protest, like someone who had accepted that some journeys, no matter how hard, couldn't be avoided.

I crouched beside the carrier, one hand resting on the cold metal grate. "See you later, mate," I whispered. "Don't flirt with the vet nurse too much."

He blinked at me, that slow, regal blink of his — the one that always said *You worry too much.*

Mrs. Patterson gave a brisk nod and lifted the carrier. "We'll be back soon," she promised. But I saw the tightness around her mouth, the way she held her breath before stepping out into the grey morning.

My stomach dropped. " Let us know what they say."

She nodded as if she already knew the answer.

I watched the car pull away and felt something uncoil in my chest — fear disguised as practicality. I tried to busy myself — medication rounds, staff paperwork, a call with the district nurse — but it all blurred into white noise. Every ring of the phone made my stomach lurch.

When Mrs. Patterson finally called a couple of hours

later, her voice told me everything before her words did.

"They've found a mass," she said quietly. "In his abdomen. The vet thinks it's cancer."

The word landed like a stone in water, sending ripples through everything. *Cancer.* Not Kev.

"How bad?" My voice didn't sound like my own.

"They need to do more tests, but… the vet thinks he's probably got a few months, maybe six if we're lucky. They could operate, but at his age, with his history…" She paused. "It might not be fair to put him through that. I'm so sorry, love. I know how much he means to you. To all of you."

I sat down, staring at nothing. *Six months.* The words wouldn't stick. My brain kept rejecting them like a faulty puzzle piece. Six months wasn't enough. Six years wouldn't have been. And that was if we were *lucky*.

"What do we do?" I finally asked.

"We keep him comfortable. The vet assured me he's not in pain right now, and he might not be for a while. So for now, he can still enjoy his life. He can keep doing his visits if he wants to. We can manage his symptoms with medication and keep him comfortable for a while. But the moment he stops eating, seems restless, or shows signs of discomfort, we'll know it's time."

I knew immediately what she meant. "We can't let him suffer," I said firmly.

Mrs P sighed. "When he's no longer enjoying his days, that's when we'll know it's time to let him go."

Let him go? How could I possibly do that? The thought was unbearable but so was the thought of him suffering just so we could have a little more time with him.

When the call ended, I stayed in my office long after the line went dead, listening to the hum of the electric wallclock and the rain ticking against the window. Then I did the only thing I knew how to do when something felt impossible — I made a plan.

Kev, the Care Home Cat

We'd tell the staff. Then, when the time came, the residents.

That afternoon's staff meeting felt heavier than any inspection debrief or safeguarding review I'd ever held. Denise was the first to cry, silent tears sliding down her plump cheeks as I explained. Even in grief, she was the same Denise—brash, loyal, and fiercely protective of everyone in this place. Alicia's jaw trembled. Even Claire, who could usually compartmentalise anything, had to leave halfway through.

"How long?" Denise asked eventually.

"Six months tops, they think."

"And he's defo not suffering?"

"Not yet. And here's the thing, he may never be. Mrs. Patterson will keep a close eye on him too, take him in for regular check ups. I'll pay of course—"

'No!" insisted Denise. "We all will—"

I held up my hand to stop her protests, pressing on. "And if Kev starts declining, if he seems like he's suffering, then we'll..." I couldn't say it. I took a deep breath. "If it comes to it—if he starts to struggle—we'll make sure he's not in pain. Not ever."

But as long as he was still Kev, still enjoying his visits, we'd keep going for as long as his little body would hold out.

***

I sat across from Adam at the kitchen table, the steam from our fish and chips supper curling into the cool evening air. I'd been dreading this conversation all day, rehearsing the words in my head over and over. Phoning or texting him with the news hadn't felt right—this needed to be done face-to-face. But now that the moment was here, the words felt heavy, clumsy, and utterly inadequate.

"Adam," I began, my voice barely above a whisper, "there's something I need to tell you."

He looked up from his plate, a chip poised halfway to his mouth. His brow furrowed at the tone of my voice. "What's wrong?"

I took a deep breath, my chest tight. "It's about Kev. He... he's not well. Mrs Patterson took him to the vets today. They found a tumour."

Adam froze, his hand hovering in midair. "A tumour?" he repeated, his voice flat, as if the word didn't quite make sense.

I nodded, my throat constricting. "It's... it's not something they can fix. He's not in pain right now, but... it's only a matter of time before—." My face crumpled.

The silence that followed was thick, suffocating. Adam set his fork down carefully, his hands trembling ever so slightly. "How long?" he finally asked, his voice cracking on the words.

"They're not sure," I replied, my own voice breaking. "A few months, maybe six."

Adam stared at the table, his jaw clenched, his eyes glassy. He looked as though he were holding himself together by sheer willpower. When he finally spoke, his voice was raw, stripped bare. "There are cats, and there are cats. He's extraordinary. He's not supposed to... he's not supposed to go like this."

"I know," I whispered, tears spilling down my cheeks. "I know."

Adam pushed his chair back abruptly and stood, pacing the room. His hands raked through his hair, his breath coming in short, uneven bursts. "What are we supposed to do? Just... just wait? Just watch him fade away?"

I stood too, crossing the room to him. I reached out, placing a hand on his arm, but he pulled away, his shoulders tense.

"We'll make his days count," I said softly, echoing Mrs P's earlier words. "However long he's got, we'll make sure he knows how much he's loved. We'll make sure he's happy."

Adam stopped pacing, his back to me. For a long moment, he didn't move. Then, with a shuddering breath, he turned and pulled me into a tight embrace, his face buried in my shoulder.

"He's the best cat," he choked out, his voice muffled. "The best damn cat."

I held him tightly, my own tears mingling with his. "I know," I whispered. "I know."

***

Christmas in a care home is controlled chaos disguised as cheer. Tinsel on mobility aids, mince pies everywhere, and at least three residents claiming to be in charge of the decorations.

It started in November with the decorations debate—who's in charge, what goes where, whether tinsel is tasteful or tacky (Florence says tacky, everyone else overrules her). Then there's the music (only carols written before 1960, according to Bert), the menu planning (traditional with accommodations for seven different dietary requirements), and the eternal question of whether the tree should be real or artificial.

"Real smells better," Maureen argued.

"Artificial doesn't drop needles everywhere," countered Florence practically.

We compromised: artificial tree, real pine branches in vases for the smell. Democracy in action.

This year, we'd decided on a full nativity scene. Denise found a plastic baby Jesus in the attic, slightly melted from years of radiator storage, and arranged him with care along with the other plastic figures. She set it up on a table in the lounge with the care of someone arranging priceless artefacts.

"There," she said, stepping back to admire her work.

"Perfect."

It lasted exactly eighteen hours.

The next morning, baby Jesus was missing.

"Who's taken the baby Jesus?" Denise demanded, hands on hips, surveying the lounge like a detective at a crime scene.

Nobody knew. Nobody had seen anything. Baby Jesus had simply vanished overnight.

We searched everywhere. Behind radiators, under chairs, in the magazine rack. Nothing.

"Maybe he's been raptured," suggested Arthur unhelpfully.

"Baby Jesus doesn't get raptured, he does the rapturing," Florence corrected. "Get your theology right."

By lunchtime, we'd given up. Baby Jesus was gone. The nativity scene looked bereft—Mary and Joseph staring forlornly at an empty manger, the shepherds pointing at nothing.

"It's like a metaphor for something," Denise mused. "But I'm not sure what."

Then Arthur called out from the conservatory: "You might want to see this."

We all trooped over. And there, under the Christmas tree, was Kev. Sprawled on his side, one paw draped protectively around the missing baby Jesus, purring with unmistakable pride and satisfaction.

There was a moment of stunned silence.

Then Maureen started laughing. Properly laughing, the kind that's infectious. Within seconds, we were all at it—even Bert, who claimed to find nothing funny about blasphemy.

"The cat's found religion," Denise managed between giggles.

Kev, unbothered by the attention, continued purring. Baby Jesus looked no worse for his relocation, though he now bore tiny teeth marks on one arm.

"Should we move Jesus back?" Grace asked.

"Absolutely not," Florence declared. "The cat's made his decision. Who are we to interfere with divine providence?"

So baby Jesus stayed under the Christmas tree. Kev appointed himself guardian, sleeping beside the nativity scene during his visits, occasionally rearranging the shepherds with a lazy paw when they weren't facing the right direction.

Visitors loved it. Families would come, see Kev and his charge, and laugh.

"Is that the therapy cat?" one woman asked.

"That's him. Currently moonlighting as a shepherd. Or possibly a wise man. We're not entirely clear on his theology."

The residents started calling him Saint Kev of Rivermead. He accepted the title with his usual grace, which is to say he ignored it entirely and continued doing exactly what he wanted. Many days, apart from his being a bit skinnier around the haunches, you wouldn't have even known he was ill.

On Christmas Eve, we gathered in the lounge for carols. The room was warm, softly lit, fairy lights twinkling on the tree, Kev pausing to sniff at a stray sprig of holly on the floor. Bert wore a paper crown and pretended not to enjoy it.

Adam stood at my side in the naffest Christmas jumper imaginable, one that practically shouted, "I'm a teacher!" without him having to say it. Mrs Patterson was also there, wearing a seasonally-themed cat sweater and flashing reindeer antlers.

We sang the old songs. "Silent Night." "O Come All Ye Faithful." "Away in a Manger." Voices wavering but sincere, Grace managing a few words of each verse, Bert humming tunelessly but with commitment.

Kev lay under the tree through it all, beside his nativity scene, eyes half-closed. When we reached "Silent Night," he opened them fully and watched us with that unnervingly attentive gaze he sometimes had.

"All is calm, all is bright," we sang, the words taking on weight in this room full of people who'd seen so many Christmases, who'd lost so much, who were facing what might be their last. And Kev who seemed to be getting thinner by the day and was definitely facing his last.

When we reached the final verse, Kev stood up. Stretched elaborately. Looked at us all gathered there—residents, staff, families—and gave one deep, contented purr that seemed to fill the entire room.

Then he walked to the centre of the circle we'd formed, sat down, and closed his eyes. Just sat there, peaceful and present, like he was blessing us all.

Nobody spoke. We just stood there in the glow of the Christmas lights, this strange collection of people and one ginger cat, and felt—what? Hope? Peace? The sense that despite everything, we were exactly where we needed to be?

"He's saying grace," Maureen whispered.

Maybe he was. Or maybe he was just being Kev—showing up, being present, reminding us that holiness looks like this: messy, imperfect, covered in cat hair, but real. So real.

After the carols, after the residents had gone to bed and the building had settled into its night-time quiet, I found Denise sitting in the lounge, just her and Kev and the Christmas tree.

"You alright?" I asked.

"Just thinking. About how this is probably my favourite Christmas I've had here. And it's entirely because of a cat stealing baby Jesus and refusing to give him back."

"It's been a good year."

"It has. Because of him." She nodded at Kev, who was back under the tree, guarding. "Everything changed when he showed up. This place, the residents, us. All better. All more... I don't know. Human?"

"More human because of a cat. That's ironic."

"That's Kev." She stood, stretched. "I'm heading home. You both should too. It's late."

After she left, Adam and I sat for a while with Kev and the tree and baby Jesus. Outside, the first snowflakes of the season began to fall, dusting the world in a quiet, peaceful white. Inside, the building breathed its sleeping breath—occasional sounds from upstairs, the heating clicking, the soft hum of machinery keeping everyone alive and comfortable.

"Thank you," I told Kev. "For this year. For everything."

He opened one eye, gave me that slow blink that meant acknowledgment, then went back to sleep.

I wrote in the Good Book:

December 24th:

Christmas Eve. Kev stole baby Jesus from the nativity scene and appointed himself guardian angel. Spent the day under the tree, protecting his charge, occasionally rearranging shepherds. During carols, he sat in the middle of our circle and purred—the sound filling the room like a benediction.

Denise said this was her favourite Christmas here. Mine too. Not because of fancy decorations or expensive presents, but because of a cat who understands that the sacred is found in small things. In showing up. In staying. In the simple act of being present with people who need you.

If Christmas is about incarnation—God becoming flesh, becoming real, becoming here—then maybe Kev is the most Christmas thing we have. Not theological, not symbolic, just furry and warm and absolutely, undeniably present.

Merry Christmas, Kev. Thank you for being here. For choosing us. For teaching us that holiness wears orange fur and steals nativity figures and purrs contentment into rooms full of people who thought they'd forgotten how to feel it.

On Christmas morning, before the residents woke, I found a small gift by the tree. Hand-wrapped, no tag. Inside was a tiny knitted mouse—orange wool, uneven stitching, clearly handmade. *For Kev.*

I never found out who made it. It didn't matter. What mattered was that someone—or several someones—had sat up late, arthritic hands working wool, making a gift for a cat who'd given them so much.

I hung it on the tree near where Kev slept. He batted at it once, decided it was acceptable, and went back to guarding baby Jesus.

Perfect. Exactly as it should be.

Christmas at Rivermead. Chaotic and beautiful and ridiculous and holy. All at once.

Just like Kev.

***

On Boxing Day, when Kev padded through the French doors, I saw it—a subtle change. His movements were slower, his jumps more measured. Still graceful, still proud, but quieter. The spark hadn't gone; it had simply shifted, softer now, like candlelight instead of flame.

He made his rounds anyway, greeting everyone in his unhurried way. When he reached Bert's chair, he hopped up with visible effort and settled into his lap.

"You alright, cat?" Bert asked, voice gentler than I'd ever heard it.

Kev gave a single mrow, his voice steady and soothing as it always was.

"Good. Don't go dying on me," Bert muttered, his eyes fixed on the newspaper in his hands, though it was clear he wasn't reading a word. "I'm too old to train another one."

I turned away before he could see my face.

***

There's a peculiar kind of cruelty in knowing. In having the diagnosis, the timeline, the countdown. Some people claim they'd want to know, but I'm not so sure. Knowing means watching. Measuring every breath, every moment, against the dwindling days. It means seeing the decline instead of simply living. But it also means this: we got to say thank you. We got to tell Kev what he meant before it was too late.

So maybe knowing is its own kind of gift. A terrible, bittersweet gift, but a gift nonetheless.

The weeks that followed were a mosaic of light and shadow—good days and quieter days, moments of warmth and stretches of stillness. Kev still came, still made his rounds from lap to lap, though sometimes he lingered by the radiator, content to simply watch the room.

The residents seemed to sense the shift without needing words. They spoke to him more softly, reached out less often, as if they, too, understood we were living on borrowed time.

We watched him like hawks, tracking every movement, every meal. Claire kept a notebook, meticulously jotting down how much he ate, how often he purred, how long he slept. Denise checked on him almost hourly, her quiet vigilance ensuring he wasn't hiding any pain.

"He's still Kev," she said one afternoon, her hand resting gently on his back as he dozed in her lap. "He's just… slower now."

But we all knew the signs. When he stopped leaping onto windowsills, when he left his favourite treats untouched, when he began to spend more time sleeping than awake—we knew the end was near.

"We're not keeping him here for us," I told the staff one evening, my voice steady despite the ache in my chest. "The moment he's not enjoying his life, we'll let him go. That's the promise we made."

***

We were taking the last of the Christmas decorations

down when Maureen broke the silence that had settled over the room. Her voice was soft but insistent, as if she were voicing the question everyone else had been too hesitant to ask.

"Is Kev alright?" she murmured, her gaze dropping to where he lay curled on her lap. "He seems… different."

I paused, the weight of the truth pressing against my chest. Lying didn't feel right, but the words were hard to say. "He's not well," I finally replied, keeping my tone gentle. "They found a tumour. He's not in pain, but… it won't get better."

Maureen's hand froze mid-stroke, her fingers resting lightly on his fur. "How long?"

"They're not sure. A few months, maybe longer."

She nodded slowly, her hand resuming its rhythmic motion. "Then we'll make it count."

"Make what count?"

"The time," she said, her voice steady but tinged with emotion. "However long he's got. I'd want to make sure he knows how loved he is. That he mattered."

I swallowed hard, my throat tightening. "He knows, Maureen. He wouldn't keep coming here if he didn't."

A small, bittersweet smile touched her lips, her eyes glistening with unshed tears. "He always did know his own mind."

Behind us, the fairy lights twinkled softly, casting one last warm glow over the room before being switched off. I hadn't wanted the residents to find out, not now, not at Christmas. But there was a quiet resolve in Maureen's words, a determination to cherish whatever time was left. And somehow, in that moment, it felt like the most fitting way to begin the New Year — with love, honesty, and the promise to make every moment matter.

Word spread gently, person to person, like a candle being passed hand to hand. I told those who needed to know —

Bert, Mabel, Florence, Grace, Arthur — one by one, in quiet corners and soft tones.

Mabel sobbed, silently. Grace swore — loudly, creatively, and with surprising fluency for someone still recovering her words after a stroke. ("That's *shit*, that is. Proper *shit*.") Arthur simply nodded, his gnarled hand resting on Kev's back. "We're all getting old, boy," he said softly. "You're in good company."

But it was Bert who broke me.

I found him in his room after Kev had gone home for the evening, staring at an old photograph — a young man in uniform, impossibly proud.

"The cat's dying," he said flatly. Not a question. A statement.

"Yes," I said quietly. "He is."

He let out a rough laugh that wasn't really laughter. "Fucking typical. You finally find someone who isn't useless, and they go and die on you."

"I'm sorry."

"Not your fault. Just life. Life's a bastard." He set the photograph down carefully. "I've outlived everyone, you know. My wife. My mates. And now the cat. My bloody cat."

"He's still here, Bert. He's still coming."

"For now." His eyes met mine, startlingly blue even at eighty-eight. "I don't know how many more goodbyes I've got in me. Thought I was done with that."

"You don't have to say goodbye yet."

"But I will." His voice cracked. "And it'll hurt. Because he's my friend. Haven't had one of those in years."

I couldn't speak. There was nothing to say that would make it easier, for either of us.

When I finally left his room, the corridor felt too long, too quiet.

"Time," Bert echoed bitterly. "Never enough of that, is there?"

I stood in the corridor for a moment, composing myself. Then I went to my office and wrote in the Good Book:
Good Book: —

> *Kev's purpose isn't measured in years. It's measured in moments. He's taught us all how to live with intention. Now he's going to teach us how to die with dignity. One last lesson from our ginger professor.*

* * *

The new year seemed to settle over us like a heavy blanket, and with it came a quiet knowing that things were changing.

The cold seemed to seep into everything that month—walls, bones, hearts—and perhaps, in its own way, into Kev too.

The vet had been clear: Kev wasn't in acute distress yet, but his body was fighting a battle it would eventually lose. Some days would be better than others. We needed to be flexible—willing to adapt to his rhythm, not ours.

So we adapted.

On his bright days, when he arrived with that familiar spring in his step and his tail held high, we let him do his full rounds—greeting everyone, collecting affection, accepting offerings of Dreamies and devotion.

On his quieter days, we set up a gentler space for him—usually the small sitting room off the main lounge—soft light, calm voices, one or two visitors at a time. Residents came in small groups then, speaking in low tones, as though in a chapel.

They understood, instinctively. After so long with Kev, they had learned to read him as fluently as he read them—the angle of his ears, the weight of his blink, the subtle flick of his tail that said *enough for now* or *yes, you can sit closer*.

It was Maureen who came up with the idea for a rotation

Kev, the Care Home Cat

schedule.

"We all want time with him," she said during a residents' meeting. "But he can't be everywhere at once anymore, especially now. What if we took turns? Gave him rest between visits?"

It was so sensible, so kind, that I felt foolish for not thinking of it first. So we drew up a chart and pinned it to the noticeboard by the lounge door. Mondays: Maureen first, then Florence, then Margaret, then open visits. Tuesdays: Bert—always Bert first, that was non-negotiable—then Grace, then Arthur, then whoever else Kev chose to grace with his company.

Other days followed a similar routine. Mabel, Denis, Agnes, Joyce, William, Harry, Millie.

Janet wasn't on the official schedule; dementia made time meaningless for her. But Kev always found her anyway. He'd slip into her room while she hummed to herself, curl up beside her armchair, and listen as she told the same story three times over. He never seemed to mind the repetition.

What surprised me most was how seriously the residents took this new system. They prepared for their time with Kev as though for a cherished appointment.

Maureen would have her favourite chair ready, a few scraps of conversation saved for him. Bert folded his newspaper precisely, marking the articles he wanted to "discuss."

"He deserves our best," Arthur said when I commented on it. "Doesn't matter that he's a cat. Doesn't matter that he doesn't understand every word. He listens. He cares. So we should care back. We should be intentional about the time we have."

That phrase stayed with me.

One day near the end of January, I saw something that stopped me in my tracks. It was the moment I truly understood just how deeply Kev had stitched himself into

171

the fabric of Rivermead.

Florence—brittle, defensive Florence, whose sharp words had once made new carers cry—was having a bad day. Her daughter had phoned to say she couldn't come for her birthday. She lived far away now; visits were rare, always deferred by "soon, if things quieten down."

Florence had hung up pretending not to care, but her hands shook as she folded her cardigan. Hurt poured off her like static.

Kev arrived that afternoon, slow but determined, his tail held like a question mark. He made his usual rounds—Grace, then Arthur, then Bert—but when he reached the doorway to the lounge, he stopped. His eyes found Florence sitting alone by the window, arms crossed, jaw tight.

It wasn't her turn. But Kev ignored the chart. He padded straight across the carpet to Florence's chair and sat at her feet.

"Go away," she said automatically. "It's not my time with you."

Kev didn't move.

"I said—" She stopped, looked down properly for the first time. "Oh, don't tell me you can tell I'm upset. You're a cat, not a therapist."

Kev gave a soft mrow, the sound small but insistent.

Florence stared at him, her face trembling in the tension between anger and surrender. Then, with a sigh that seemed to come from somewhere far deeper than her lungs, she bent and lifted him. Her movements were clumsy—she wasn't used to holding him—but Kev adjusted, settling into her arms with a patience that looked almost holy.

"My daughter's not coming," Florence said quietly. "Again. She's busy, of course she is. She has her own life. I understand that. But I'm her mother. Doesn't that count for something?"

Kev pushed his head beneath her chin and purred. The

sound filled the space like warmth.

"I've been awful," she whispered, the words cracking. "To everyone here. To you, at first. I've been angry because I'm scared. Scared of being useless. Of being left behind. But being awful doesn't make me less lonely—it just makes me impossible to love."

Her tears fell onto his fur, and he didn't flinch.

"Except maybe you," she said, voice shaking. "You'd miss me, wouldn't you? Even after all that?"

Kev purred harder, an unambiguous yes.

I stood at the doorway, hardly breathing. The faint whiff of disinfectant and brewing tea hung in the air, as familiar as the home itself. Across the room, one of the other residents had appeared—her turn, technically—but when she saw what was happening, she caught my eye and shook her head gently. *Leave them. This matters more.*

Florence sat like that for nearly an hour. When she finally placed Kev back on his blanket, her face was red and blotchy from crying, but her shoulders looked lighter, looser.

"Thank you," she whispered to him. "For being patient with me. For not giving up."

After that day, Florence changed. Not completely—she was still Florence, still sharp and opinionated—but the bitterness was gone. She joined group activities again, sometimes even started them. She complimented Denise's baking. She laughed at Arthur's jokes. Once, she even thanked a junior carer for bringing her tea.

"The cat fixed her," Denise said, half-joking.

"The cat gave her permission to be vulnerable," I said. "That's not the same as being fixed. But it's a start."

Good Book —

Kev with Florence today. Witnessed something close to a miracle. She's been living in armour for years, and somehow he just... walked through it. No fanfare, no effort, just presence. I don't know how he does it, how he knows exactly who needs him and when. Maybe it's instinct. Maybe it's grace. Either way, I'm grateful—for the questions, for the mystery, for Kev.

* * *

Snowdrops were just breaking through the earth outside the lounge window, their faint scent mingling with the morning's chaos when I found Maureen crying in the lounge, her hand resting on Kev's empty blanket.

"He's not gone yet," she said, voice trembling, "and I'm already mourning him."

"We all are," I said softly, sitting beside her. "We're mourning Kev together. Knowing what's coming—it makes it harder and easier at the same time."

She gave a small, broken laugh. "I keep thinking about Harold's last months. How I didn't know they were his last. I didn't know to pay attention—to memorise things. And now, with Kev, we know. We can prepare. But it doesn't feel like a gift." She wiped her eyes. "It feels like torture."

"It's both," I said quietly. "That's what makes it so hard."

We sat in silence for a while, watching rain chase itself down the windows. The air hummed faintly with the sound of the heating pipes and distant chatter from the corridor. It felt like the whole home was holding its breath.

After a moment, Maureen spoke again. "I wrote him a letter," she said. "Telling him everything he's meant to me. But I can't give it to him—he can't read. And I can't give it to Mrs. Patterson—it's too personal. So it's just sitting there, in my Memory Box. A love letter to a cat that no one will ever read."

The Memory Box had become its own quiet ritual. Residents slipped notes into it now and then—birthday cards, prayers, fragments of poems, folded sheets of stationery perfumed with lavender. On rainy days, there always seemed to be one or two more, tucked in anonymously. It was our shared act of reverence.

"I'll read it," I offered. "If you want someone to witness it."

She hesitated, then nodded. "Yes. I think I'd like that."

She disappeared for a moment and came back holding three pages of paper, filled margin to margin in tiny, careful handwriting.

I read it there in the lounge while she watched my face. It was beautiful—and devastating.

She wrote about Harold, about the raw edges of grief and the morning she'd woken up thinking *I can't do another day*, only to see Kev waiting at the French windows. She wrote that his presence had been the difference between surviving and giving up.

She wrote that love doesn't heal you—it just makes the brokenness bearable.

When I finished, I had to wipe my eyes. "Maureen," I said hoarsely, "this is extraordinary."

"It's just the truth."

"Would you let me photocopy it? I'd like to add it to Kev's file. Not for publicity—just so people in other care homes, people making decisions about therapy animals, can see what this really means. Not statistics. Not tick boxes. The *real* impact."

She smiled through her tears. "If it helps someone else say yes to their own Kev, then yes. Use it."

Word spread, as it always did, and over the following days, other residents began to ask if they could share their letters too. So that Saturday, grey and drizzly, we gathered in the lounge—residents, staff, a circle of chairs and tissues. One by one, they read.

Mabel went first. Her voice shook as she read a letter to her late sister, telling her about "this remarkable cat who visits us," and how she wished her sister could have met him.

Grace read hers haltingly, her words coming slow but steady, a letter to her younger self:

You will lose so much—your words, your independence, your certainty. But one day, a scruffy cat will curl up on your lap and remind you that love doesn't need perfect sentences.

Arthur's was addressed to his late wife:

Remember how you always wanted a cat, and I said no because of my allergies? Well, I found a way. Better late than never.

And even Florence—sharp-tongued, fiercely private Florence—read hers aloud. A letter to her daughter so far away from her:

I've been angry for so long. At you for leaving, at myself for needing help, at the world for moving on without my permission. But this cat doesn't care about my anger. He just sits with me anyway. I'm trying to learn from him—to just sit with people without demanding they be perfect first. I'm not there yet. But I'm trying.

By the end, there wasn't a dry eye in the room—residents, carers, even Bert, who claimed he was "allergic to sentiment" but still kept blowing his nose. The letters had turned into something bigger than grief: a celebration of what Kev had given us while he was still here. A living memorial, offered in advance.

That night, while organising the letters in the box, I found one I hadn't seen before. No name. Just shaky handwriting on plain notepaper:

Dear God, or Universe, or Whatever's Listening,
Thank you for the cat.
I don't believe in much anymore.
I've watched too many people die, seen too much that prayer couldn't fix. But that cat feels like grace.
Like proof that something, somewhere, sometimes gets it right.
If you're up there—if you're real—send more cats.
Send them to every care home, every hospital, every place where people are dying slowly and need something to live for, even if it's just two

Kev, the Care Home Cat

o'clock each afternoon.
We don't need miracles.
We just need small mercies.
We just need Kev.
Amen, or whatever you say when you're not sure anyone's listening.

I never found out who wrote it. But I kept it at the front of the box. Because it felt, somehow, like the truest prayer I'd ever read.

***

January bled into February, and with it came a strange urgency. Not panic—we'd moved past panic into something else. Acceptance, maybe, mixed with desperate gratitude for every day Kev still came, still purred, still chose to be with us.

Despite the promise of Spring in the air, the days were the kind where it's dark when you arrive at work and dark when you leave. The heating struggled against the cold, and frost etched patterns on the windows every morning that didn't melt until noon, if at all.

Kev would sit by the radiator, eyes half-closed, while the residents talked around him. It reminded me of an old general at a reunion — too tired to lead the parade, but still the centre of it.

Mrs. Patterson and I had agreed to monitor things quietly. So we waited. Not for the end, exactly, but for the moment when the joy would stop outweighing the effort. Until then, Kev was still ours, and we were still his.

Bert tried to pretend nothing was wrong. He'd read his paper out loud to Kev, pausing to grumble about the government, the football scores, the price of milk. Kev would sit in his lap and listen, eyes half-closed, tail occasionally flicking as if in commentary.

One morning, Bert caught me watching them from the

doorway. "Don't look at me like that," he said. "He's not gone yet."

"I know."

'Don't worry,' Bert said gruffly. 'He's just conserving energy. Probably planning his next heist—baby Jesus, Part Two for Easter.'"

I laughed despite the sadness weighing down my heart. Somehow knowing Kev wouldn't make Easter.

"He hates pity."

"I know that too."

He gave a small grunt of approval and went back to his reading. Still, later that night, I saw him slip Kev a piece of smoked haddock from his dinner tray — against all dietary rules — and whisper, "Don't tell the nurses."

Good Book —

Kev slower this week. Still alert, still purring. The residents orbit him like planets around a fading sun. It's not sadness exactly — more like reverence. As if they're all remembering what he's done for them and trying to return the favour.

Watching him, I couldn't help but feel a pang of sadness. He'd given so much to this place, to all of us, and now it's our turn to care for him. Not that he is not always still ministering to us all in his furry purry way.

***

The vet had said six months, perhaps—but before three had passed, we knew we wouldn't have that long. Kev was slowing, drawing inward, guarding what little strength remained. Each day he seemed to grow fainter, the edges of his presence softening like fading sunlight.

The lively rounds he once made—his cheerful inspections, his unhurried greetings—had become brief wanderings, small echoes of the life that had filled every corner of the place. The vet adjusted his pain relief, gentle mercy in tiny doses, and we understood what lay ahead. There would come a day when comfort could no longer keep pace with his courage, and we would have to do the hardest, kindest thing—let this magnificent spirit go.

It was Bert who finally said what we were all thinking.

"Will you tell us? Before... before you have to put him down?"

The question hit like a punch. "If we can. If there's time."

"I want to say goodbye properly," he said fiercely. "Not like everyone else—one day here, next day gone. I want to *know*."

"I'll make sure you can," I promised, though I wasn't certain I could keep it. Cats don't schedule their endings. "If it's at all possible."

Kev slept more. Sometimes he'd curl up in Maureen's lap and barely stir for an hour. Other times he'd wedge himself under the piano stool, the way cats do when they're looking for comfort they can't quite ask for.

Once, when I was locking up the medicine cabinet, I caught Denise watching him with tears in her eyes.

"Reminds me of my dad," she said quietly. "When he got ill. You could tell he was ready to go before any of us were. Stopped fussing, stopped pretending. Just wanted everyone to sit with him, not talk too much."

I nodded. "Kev's like that. Doesn't need noise. Just company."

"Then that's what we'll give him," she said.

***

We didn't plan the day the goodbye began — it just arrived.

It was a Wednesday in February, a week before Valentine's Day, the first sunlight of the year filled with the promise of Spring slipping through the blinds. Mrs.

Patterson phoned me that morning: "He's not eaten since yesterday. He'd barely moved from his bed, He's still purring, but... slower. It's not fair to make him hold on any longer."

My heart dropped. "When?"

"Tomorrow morning. Ten o'clock. It'll be peaceful. He'll just go to sleep." Her voice was rough with tears. "I think he'd like to see everyone before then."

I swallowed the lump in my throat. "Bring him."

After we hung up, I sat in my office with my head in my hands. Tomorrow. We had until tomorrow.

I gathered the staff. Told them as gently as I could. Denise broke first, then Alicia, then even unshakable Claire.

"Do we tell the residents?" Denise asked.

"Yes. They deserve to know. And..." I swallowed hard. "Mrs Patterson's agreed to something. If anyone wants to say goodbye, she'll bring him here first. One last visit."

"Oh, God," Denise whispered. "That's going to destroy them."

"I know. But it's only right. They need to say goodbye."

We met in the lounge after dinner—everyone who'd known him, loved him, been changed by him. The room was full, but silent.

"I have some difficult news," I began—and had to pause, to find my breath, to steady the tremor in my voice. The tears gathered but I held them back, just barely.

"Kev's very ill now. The vet says his pain can't be managed anymore, and it wouldn't be kind to let him go on suffering. Tomorrow morning... they'll help him go to sleep, peacefully, so he doesn't hurt anymore."

The last words tumbled out too fast, as if rushing them might somehow make them less real.

For a long time there was no sound at all. Then Maureen gave a small animal-like cry and buried her face in her hands.

"No," Grace said clearly. "No, that's wrong."

"I'm so sorry," I said, tears running freely now. "I wish there was another way."

"What time?" Arthur asked.

"Ten, tomorrow morning. But Mrs Patterson will bring him here first, so you can say your goodbyes. Just for a little while. He's very tired. It wouldn't be fair."

"I want to," Bert said immediately. "I *need* to."

"Me too," Maureen whispered.

"All of us," Florence added. "He'd want all of us there."

So it was decided. Tomorrow at nine o'clock, Kev would come to Rivermead for one last time.

***

The morning arrived pale and reluctant, faint sunshine breaking through thin cloud like something apologetic.

I'd been awake since four, lying in Adam's arms and listening to his steady breathing, unable to shake the feeling that the world was about to tilt and never quite right itself again.

"You should try to sleep," he'd murmured around five, proving he'd been awake too.

"Can't."

"I know." He'd held me tighter. "I'll be there with you. Every minute."

"You don't have to—"

"Dawn." His voice was firm but gentle. "Stop. I'm coming. We're doing this together."

By eight o'clock, we were at Rivermead. The building was too quiet, even the usual morning sounds muted—as if the walls themselves were holding their breath. The air tasted of the too-strong coffee someone had made, bitter and urgent.

The building felt different already—heavier, somehow, as if grief had weight and was pressing down on the roof, seeping through the walls.

The staff were there early too. Denise had made tea no one would drink. Claire had rearranged the lounge chairs three times. Alicia kept checking the thermostat, convinced the room was too cold, then too warm, unable to settle because settling meant accepting what was about to happen.

Ruth and Sasha, despite being desperate for sleep, had stayed on after night shift to say their goodbyes.

Adam made himself useful in the way he'd learned over the past months—quietly, without fuss. Made fresh tea when the first pot went cold—even though nobody drank it. Helped Arthur get comfortable in his chair. Held tissues ready for when—not if, but when—they'd be needed.

The residents had begun gathering at half past eight. No one had needed calling. They'd simply appeared, dressed in their best—the clothes reserved for important occasions, for days that would be remembered.

Grace wore the cardigan her daughter had given her last Christmas. Arthur had put on a tie. Bert his military blazer.

They arranged themselves in a loose semicircle, leaving the centre space empty. Waiting.

"She'll bring him soon," I told them, checking my watch for the hundredth time. Quarter to nine. Fifteen minutes.

"We're ready," Maureen said, though her hands were shaking as she smoothed her skirt. "As ready as we can be."

Adam appeared at my elbow with a mug of tea I didn't remember asking for. "Drink," he said quietly. "You need it."

"I'm fine."

"You're not fine. Neither am I. Neither is anyone. But you still need tea."

I took it, grateful for something to do with my hands, and he stayed beside me, solid and steady and exactly where I needed him to be.

At ten to nine, Mrs. Patterson's car pulled up outside.

The conversation in the lounge died instantly. Everyone turned toward the French windows, watching as she opened the back door and carefully lifted out the small carrier.

"Oh God," Denise whispered behind me. "I thought I was ready. I'm not ready."

"None of us are," Adam said gently, and I felt his hand find mine, fingers lacing together. Anchoring me.

Mrs. Patterson came through the main entrance, and I met her in the corridor. Her eyes were red, face puffy from crying, but she was composed. Determined to do this right.

"He's had his pain medication," she said quietly. "He's comfortable. Not in any distress. But he's very weak. He won't be able to walk much."

"We'll carry him. Whatever he needs."

She nodded, then looked past me to the lounge full of waiting residents. "They all want to say goodbye?"

"Every single one."

"Then let's not keep them waiting." Her voice cracked slightly. "He'd hate that. Always impatient, our Kev."

Together we walked into the lounge, Adam following close behind. The residents that could stood as we entered, a mark of respect that made my throat close up.

I set the carrier on the low table in the centre of their circle and opened the door.

For a moment, Kev didn't emerge. Just sat inside, amber eyes taking in the scene—all these people gathered, all this love focused on him. Then, slowly, he stepped out onto the table.

Someone gasped. He was so thin now, his coat dull, movements careful and deliberate. But his tail was still up, his head still high. Still Kev. Still dignified.

"Hello, boy," Bert said, his voice rough. "There you are."

Kev turned toward the sound and mrowed—soft, almost tentative, but unmistakably a greeting.

"Can we touch him?" Maureen asked.

"Of course," Mrs. Patterson said. "That's why we're here. So you can say goodbye properly."

Maureen went first. Knelt beside the table, hands trembling as she reached out to stroke his head. "Hello, my darling. Look at you. Still so handsome."

Kev pushed his head into her hand, purring—that deep, rumbling purr we'd all come to know so well. Not as strong as it once was, but still there. Still Kev.

"Thank you," Maureen whispered, tears streaming down her face. "Thank you for everything. For sitting with me when I wanted to die. For giving me reasons to wake up. For being my friend." Her voice broke. "I love you. I hope you know that. I love you so much."

Adam moved quietly around the room, tissue box in hand, offering them to residents as they needed them. Not intrusively, just there—present and useful and kind.

Grace went next, her movements slow but purposeful. She sat on the floor beside the table—no easy feat for someone still recovering from a stroke—and took Kev's face gently between her hands.

"You... gave me... words back," she said, each one carefully formed, deliberately clear. "Made me... believe... I could... speak again." She pressed her forehead to his. "Thank you... for listening. For... patience. For... everything."

Kev purred against her face, and Grace's tears fell into his fur.

Arthur wheeled his chair close. "Remember when you first came to me, boy? I told you I didn't need a cat. Told you I was fine on my own." He laughed wetly. "Turns out I was wrong about that. About a lot of things. You taught an old man it's never too late to make friends. Never too late to care."

Even Florence came forward—prickly, defensive Florence who'd spent months pretending Kev didn't matter to her.

"I don't have pretty words," she said. "I'm not good at this sort of thing. But you were patient with me when I didn't deserve it. You sat with me when I was awful. And somehow—" her voice cracked, "—somehow that made me want to be better. So thank you for that. For not giving up on me when I'd given up on myself."

One by one, they came. Each resident taking their turn, saying their piece, touching him one last time. Some spoke at length. Others just whispered "thank you" and "goodbye" through their tears.

Mabel promised she would look at the stars and think of him each night. I knew we all would in our own way.

Janet was having a confused day—Tom had warned us—but when it was her turn, something shifted in her eyes. A moment of clarity, like sun breaking through clouds.

"Kev," she said, perfectly lucid. "You're going, aren't you?"

Tom started to redirect her—"It's okay, love, he's just—"

"Don't," Janet interrupted, more forceful than I'd heard her in months. "I know what's happening. Let me say goodbye."

She knelt beside him, joints protesting, and cupped his face in her hands. "Thank you for those afternoons. Thank you for the calm. I won't remember this tomorrow—I might not remember it in an hour—but right now, I remember everything. And I'm grateful."

Kev pressed into her hands, purring, and Janet smiled through her tears before Tom helped her back to her chair.

Finally, it was Bert's turn.

He'd been sitting quietly through all of it, hands gripping his walker, jaw tight with the effort of not breaking down. Now he stood—slowly, painfully—and made his way to the table.

For a long moment, he just looked at Kev. Then he reached out one gnarled hand and began to stroke his head with a gentleness that would have surprised anyone who didn't know him.

"Right then, cat," he said, voice gruff. "I'm not good at

this. Never have been. But I want you to know—" He stopped, swallowed hard, tried again. "I want you to know you were the best friend I've had in twenty years. Since Margaret died. I thought I was done with friends. Thought I was too old, too difficult, too far gone."

Kev purred under his hand.

"But you didn't care about any of that, did you? Just showed up every afternoon like clockwork. Listened to an old man ramble about nothing. Made me feel less alone." His voice broke completely. "I'm going to miss you, boy. More than I thought possible. More than I want to admit."

He bent down—God knows what it cost his arthritic back—and pressed his face to Kev's head. "Thank you," he whispered. "You did your job, lad. Better than most humans ever could."

When he straightened, there were tears in his eyes, but he was smiling. "Right. Off you go then. You've earned your rest. Done your duty and then some."

Adam appeared at Bert's elbow, offering support as the old man made his way back to his chair. "You alright?"

"No," Bert said honestly. "But I will be. Eventually."

When all the residents had said their goodbyes, I realised it was my turn.

I knelt beside the table, and Kev turned to look at me. Those amber eyes—still bright, still knowing—seemed to see right through me.

"I don't know how to do this," I told him, voice breaking. "Don't know how to say goodbye to you. Don't know how to run this place without you."

Adam's hand found my shoulder, steady and warm.

"You changed everything, Kev. You know that? I was having the worst day of my career when you showed up. Was questioning whether I could do this job, whether any of it mattered. And then there you were, a scruffy ginger tom who decided we were worth his time."

I stroked his head, felt the familiar texture of his fur, tried to memorise every inch of it. "You taught us how to care. Really care. Not just going through the motions, but being present. Being there for people when they need you. Showing up even when it's hard—*especially* when it's hard."

Kev pushed his head into my hand, purring.

"I love you," I whispered. "We all love you. And we're going to miss you so much. But we understand. We know you're tired. We know it's time." I pressed my forehead to his. "Thank you, Kev. For everything. For choosing us. For staying as long as you could. For teaching us that love—even temporary, fragile love—is always worth it."

Behind me, Adam's hand tightened on my shoulder. When I looked up, his face was wet with tears he wasn't bothering to hide.

Mrs. Patterson checked her watch. "We should go soon," she said gently. "Dr. Morrison will be waiting."

"Can we have a few more minutes?" Maureen asked. "Please?"

"Of course."

So we sat together—all of us, residents and staff and Adam and me—in that quiet lounge while Kev lay on his blanket and purred. We told stories about him. About his first visit, his various interventions, the small miracles he'd performed just by being present.

"Remember when he stole baby Jesus?" Claire said, laughing through tears.

"Remember his midnight patrols with Mabel?" Ruth added.

"Remember how he'd sit in Dorothy's chair but never sit *in* it?" Denise said. "Like he was keeping it warm for her."

The stories poured out, each one a thread in the tapestry of what Kev had meant to us. And through it all, he lay there purring, accepting our love, our gratitude, our grief.

At twenty to ten, Mrs. Patterson stood. "It's time."

The words landed like stones in water, rippling through the room.

"No," Grace whispered. "Not yet."

"I'm sorry, love. But we can't wait any longer. It wouldn't be fair to him."

She was right. Kev was tired—visibly, terribly tired. His breathing had gotten shallower over just the past half hour. Staying longer would be selfish.

But God, it was hard to let go.

Mrs. Patterson gently lifted Kev and placed him back in his carrier. He didn't protest, just settled onto his blanket with a soft sigh.

"Goodbye, Kev," the residents chorused, voices breaking.

Denise produced Baby Jesus from her pocket and quickly stuffed it into his carrier, as if it would act as a final talisman blessing his final journey.

And just like that, Kev was gone.

Gone. Such a small word for such an enormous presence.

***

That night, back at the flat with Adam, I wrote in the Good Book one last time about Kev:

There are entries in the Good Book I still can't read without tears smudging the ink. The one that begins '*Kev didn't come back today*' is one of them.

> *Today we said goodbye to Kev.*
>
> *He died at 10:17 this morning at the vet's office. Peaceful. Pain-free. Surrounded by love. Mrs. Patterson, said he was purring right up until the end.*
>
> *The residents said goodbye properly—every single one of them. They told him what he meant to them, thanked him, cried over him, celebrated him. It was the hardest and most beautiful thing I've ever witnessed.*
>
> *I used to think love was about saving things — saving people, saving moments. But Kev taught us something*

different: love is showing up. Even when it hurts. Especially when it hurts.

Thank you, Kev. For everything. For choosing us. For staying. For teaching us that even in a place where people come to die, there's still so much life, so much love, so much worth fighting for.

Rest well, brave beautiful boy. You've earned it.

I closed the book and set it aside. Adam pulled me close, and we lay there in the dark, processing the day, processing the loss, trying to figure out how to move forward.

"We'll be okay," Adam said into my hair. "It won't feel like it for a while. But we will."

"Promise?"

"Promise. Kev made sure of that. He taught us how."

And lying there with Adam's arms around me, grief sitting heavy in my chest but love sitting heavier, I chose to believe him.

Kev had taught us many things.

But maybe the most important was this: that showing up for each other—being present through joy and grief and everything in between—that's what love looks like.

That's what matters.

That's what stays.

***

The days after Kev died were grey in a way that had nothing to do with February. The home felt quieter, emptier, as if the heart of Rivermead had skipped a beat. But even in his absence, his presence lingered—in the residents' stories, in the staff's memories.

I found Claire sitting in the garden one morning, staring at the empty patch where Kev used to sunbathe. Adam had found her first, draped his own coat over her shoulders, and was sitting beside her in the cold.

"It was just a cat," Claire said when I joined them. "I

know it's stupid to be this upset over a cat."

"It's not stupid," Adam said before I could respond. "He wasn't just a cat. He was hope. He was proof that showing up matters, that small acts of care can change everything. You learned that from him, and now you do it for the residents every single day. That's not stupid---that's legacy."

Claire wiped her eyes. "Did you just therapy-speak me?"

"Probably. Is it working?"

"A bit."

Adam caught my eye over Claire's head, and I saw my own grief reflected there—but also something steadier. A reminder that we were doing this together.

That week, Adam helped organise the small tasks that grief makes impossible. He fielded phone calls from families asking about the memorial. He coordinated with Mrs. Patterson about the ashes. He even helped Denise bake for the ceremony, standing in our tiny staff kitchen rolling pastry while she cried into the flour.

"You're better at this than I expected," Denise told him, watching him crimp the edges of a quiche.

"My mum taught me. Said if you can't cook, you can't care for people properly. Food is love, apparently."

"Your mum was right." Denise wiped her eyes. "You're good for Dawn, you know. Good for all of us."

"Kev approved," Adam said simply. "That's all the credential I need."

"Just keep on bringing cake. Or Kev will haunt you!" she laughed. And then she burst into tears and soon all the staff were bawling with her.

In the days that followed, Rivermead moved softly, as if afraid to disturb the quiet Kev had left behind. We kept busy —because that's what people do when they don't quite know what else to feel—but the silence between us spoke volumes.

Mrs Patterson came a week later, eyes still red but smiling faintly. She carried the small ceramic urn.

Kev, the Care Home Cat

"His ashes," she said. "I thought maybe you'd want to scatter them here. So he's part of this place. Always."

She sat with us in my office while we planned the memorial.

"Let's do it under the oak tree," Denise suggested quietly. "Where it's peaceful. Where people can sit and remember."

Mrs. P smiled through her tears. "He would like that."

We held a small ceremony in the garden that Friday afternoon. No hymns, no prayers—just words and presence.

Adam stood beside me throughout---solid, steady, present. When my voice failed halfway through reading from the *Good Book*, he picked up where I left off without being asked, reading Kev's story back to the people who'd lived it.

Mabel read a poem. Grace managed hers too, halting but determined, every line a triumph. Bert spoke next, a few rough words about duty and friendship and showing up, which was his way of saying love.

I decided to read some lines from Dorothy's poem, the one she'd written for Kev:

When I leave this place...
I'll visit in the sunlight if I can,
A warm breeze through the window,
A golden glow on the sill.
Look for me in the flicker of dust motes,
In the patch of sun where you nap.
I'll be the soft rustle of leaves,
The quiet hum of a lazy afternoon.

Maureen was crying openly. So was Bert, though he'd deny it later. Denise was bawling again.

When we scattered Kev's ashes, the February wind carried them beneath the great oak. The tree stood bare and still, its branches etched against a washed-out sky—seemingly lifeless, yet we knew better. It was only waiting. Beneath the bark, life was quietly gathering itself, ready to begin again when the time was right.

It felt fitting somehow—that Kev, who had made warmth from the simplest things, would rest beneath a tree that only appeared asleep, never gone.

Adam's hand found mine. His fingers laced through mine with that familiar certainty, and I felt—not okay, not healed, but less alone. Less broken.

"He should be somewhere beautiful," Maureen said quietly. "Somewhere peaceful."

"He should be *here,*" Arthur added. "With us. Where he belonged."

Denise hesitated a moment then knelt down to bury the baby Jesus Mrs P had brought back from the vets with Kev's ashes. "If heaven wanted an angel it was that cat." she said.

After everyone drifted inside, Adam and I stayed in the garden together, neither ready to leave yet. I stood by the tree and thought about that scruffy stray who'd chosen us, who'd found the broken parts of people and somehow made them whole again. Fourteen months. That's all we'd had. But what months they had been.

"Thank you," I said—to the garden, to the ashes in the soil, to the invisible presence I still felt all around. "Thank you for everything."

We turned to go back inside.

"He'd be proud of you," Adam said softly as walked down the path. "Of what you've built here. Of how you loved him. Of how you're helping everyone through this."

I leaned into him as we walked, grateful for the warmth, the solidity. "I couldn't do this without you. These past days---I would have fallen apart."

"No you wouldn't. You're much stronger than you think. But you don't have to be strong alone. That's the point." He kissed my temple. "Kev knew that. He was a cat, but he was never really alone. He had Mrs. Patterson, had all of you. Built his own family. That's what we're doing—building family from people who show up."

"Is that what we are? Family?"

"What else would you call it?"

I looked back at the building—at Rivermead, with its residents and staff and memories and grief and love all tangled together. Adam had become part of that tangle so seamlessly I couldn't remember a version of this place without him.

"Family," I agreed. "That works."

* * *

The week after we scattered Kev's ashes, something strange happened.

Residents started leaving things under the oak tree.

Maureen left a packet of Dreamies. Grace left a ball of wool—one of the ones Kev used to bat around during her speech therapy sessions. Even Bert left something: a clipping from his newspaper about therapy animals in care homes, circled in red pen.

No one talked about it. They just did it.

And the offerings accumulated. Flowers from the garden. A small toy mouse. A photograph. A letter in an envelope marked simply "Kev."

I thought about tidying them away—they'd get wet in the rain, blown about by wind. But something stopped me.

"Leave them," Adam said when I mentioned it. "It's their way of processing. Let them grieve how they need to."

So I left them. And more appeared. Cards from families thanking Kev for what he'd done for their relatives. Drawings from children who'd met him during visits.

The oak tree became a memorial without us planning it. Organic and messy and deeply human.

The offerings stayed. Through rain and wind and changing seasons. Some blew away or decomposed. Others remained, becoming part of the tree's roots, feeding it. Feeding the memory. Keeping Kev present, even in absence.

It was weeks before I stopped listening for the jingle of his collar. The home settled into its new rhythm — slower, softer — as if we were all learning to live in the silence he'd left behind.

I'd catch myself glancing toward the patio at two o'clock, expecting that familiar mrow. The silence that followed was its own kind of sermon.

But one day— someone—I don't know who—had left his collar on the windowsill, the tag glinting in the early spring sunshine.

It read: KEV — I live everywhere and nowhere. If found, I'm not lost.

And somehow, that felt exactly right.

LEGACY

Life at Rivermead carried on, because it had to. The residents still laughed, still argued over biscuits, still filled the corridors with their stories. But something lingered — a gentler patience, a habit of noticing small things. Kev had left us that.

The lounge still gets that particular quality of light around two o'clock sometimes, golden and gentle. Today, the French windows are open slightly, and I can smell the garden —autumn this time, leaf-mold and chrysanthemums. Someone's baking in the kitchen, and the scent of cinnamon drifts through. The building breathes its usual sounds: the hum of the tea urn, someone's television, the soft shuffle of slippers on linoleum.

I'll turn, half expecting to see him at the French windows, tail high, waiting to be let in with that patient certainty that he belonged here. He's not there, of course. But the memory is. The shape of him remains.

Rivermead is different now, though perhaps not in the ways you'd expect. We have a full therapy animal programme—not just cats, but dogs, rabbits, even a visiting cockatiel named Eric who swears enthusiastically - enough to make Grace blush - and makes the residents laugh. None of them are Kev. But they don't need to be. They're themselves, and that's enough.

The important thing is that we said yes. We opened the door. We took the risk. And now other animals come, other connections form, other small miracles happen.

"Do you think Kev would approve?" Adam asked last month, watching a golden retriever named Biscuit make her rounds.

"I think he'd be insufferably smug about starting a movement," I said, and he laughed.

Last spring, Adam proposed. In the garden at Rivermead, beside the oak tree, with twenty residents watching from the lounge windows and pretending they hadn't planned this ambush.

The oak tree had new leaves, fresh green against the spring sky.

"I've been thinking," Adam said, sitting on the bench beneath the tree. "About what Kev taught us. About showing up and staying and building family from the people who matter."

"Me too."

He took my hand. "I want to make it official. The staying part."

My heart jumped. "Official how?"

"The forever kind of official." He pulled a small box from his pocket, opened it. Inside was a simple solitaire ring. "I asked them first—the residents. Got their permission. Bert said if I didn't ask soon, he'd do it for me. Florence gave me advice on choosing the ring—apparently I needed proper guidance. Maureen cried for an hour when I told her I was planning it."

I was crying too, laughing and crying at once. "You asked them before me?"

"Of course. They're family. And they had opinions—extensive, conflicting opinions. But they all agreed on one thing: that Kev brought us together, and we should honour that by making it permanent."

"Yes," I said, not waiting for him to actually ask. "Yes. Obviously yes."

He slipped the ring on my finger, then kissed me while the oak tree whispered above us and somewhere in the building, residents who'd definitely been watching from the windows started cheering.

"Kev would be so smug," I said against his mouth.

"Kev would take full credit," Adam agreed. "And he'd be right to. None of this happens without him."

"No," I said, looking at the ring, at Adam, at the building full of people we loved. "None of this happens without him."

A small gust of wind rose, stirring the branches overhead. They whispered against each other, a soft rustling sound, like fur brushing past a doorway.

I chose to take it as Kev having the final word.

FINAL NOTE

This morning, before I finished writing this, I went to Kev's tree.

It's late October, eighteen months since he died. The leaves are turning, making the garden golden and rust and impossibly beautiful in that way autumn has of being gorgeous while promising death.

I sat on the bench beneath the oak—the same bench where Adam proposed, where we scattered Kev's ashes, where residents sit when they need quiet.

And I talked to him. To Kev. To the memory of him. To whatever remains when bodies are gone and all that's left is impact.

"I finished your book," I told the empty air. "I hope I did it justice. I hope I told your story the way it deserved to be told."

A breeze stirred the leaves. Nothing magical. Nothing mystical. Just wind. But I remembered the words of Dorothy's poem. *I'll be the soft rustle of leaves, the quiet hum of a lazy afternoon.*

"We're okay," I continued. "Not the same. But okay. The work continues. The doors stay open. We keep saying yes."

Another gust. Leaves spiralling down around me like benediction.

I sat there for a long time, just breathing. Just being present. Just practicing what Kev had taught me.

Finally, I stood to leave. "Thank you," I whispered. "For everything. For choosing us. For staying. For teaching us how to love temporary things."

"For showing us that temporary doesn't mean

meaningless."

"For proving that one small life can change everything."

As I walked back toward the building, I heard it. Clear as day, impossible to deny.

A mrow.

I turned.

Nothing there. Just the tree, the bench, the autumn leaves falling.

But I'd heard it. That particular sound. Kev's sound.

Maybe just memory. Maybe just grief taking auditory form. Maybe just my desperate need for closure taking the shape of cat vocalisation.

Or maybe something else.

Maybe presence that continues after bodies fail.

Maybe love that transforms but doesn't end.

Maybe Kev, keeping watch one more time.

I choose to believe the last one.

Because that's what Kev taught us: to choose hope over cynicism. Connection over safety. Love over fear.

Always love.

www.ingramcontent.com/pod-product-compliance
Lightning Source LLC
Chambersburg PA
CBHW030321080526
44584CB00012B/649